*TED DEXTER'S*
*CRICKET BOOK*

*Richie Benaud, Ted Dexter and Wally Grout during the 1961 Australian tour*

# TED DEXTER'S

## Cricket Book

ARTHUR BARKER LIMITED

20 NEW BOND STREET LONDON W1

Printed in Great Britain by D. R. Hillman & Sons Ltd., Frome

# CONTENTS

## Chapter 1

# THIS LUCKY FELLA

I PLAYED with a ball incessantly as a small boy—others could go running, tree-climbing, fighting, but I was happier throwing a ball against a wall and catching. I don't ever remember being bored by that game, and, even now, relax happily in the same way. Nobody much enjoys a game he does not play well, and my passion for throwing and catching came from a good eye for a ball.

My father was a fine athlete as a young man, and his valete from school in 1910 is almost identical to mine in 1953. The lists of school colours and rather shorter lists of other school honours run word for word. My mother is no fool on the golf course, and perhaps I was handed down some of the athletics ability of her father who represented England in at least one International Games.

It was a good pedigree for any budding cricketer, and I am grateful to them more than anyone for their unfailing support at every moment of my cricket career.

My first recollection of making a score was at the age of 9, when I scored fifty for a representative side at my Prep School, Norfolk House. I could hit the ball harder than most of my age—I hit a ball over what seemed to be tall trees on the edge of a big ground. I went back to look at that same ground, and trees, fifteen years later. It looked more like a small soccer pitch than a big cricket ground.

The war ended in time to allow a few games of soccer against Davenies and Gayhurst. They are the only memory I have of competing seriously in sport at that age. House matches were therefore the most important games of the cricket

7

season, and in one of these I made my first century at the age of 12.

My Prep School had to be closed fully a year before my intended entry to Radley. A couple of terms were spent swotting up interrupted studies before Radley kindly took me a term early. It was a summer term, and this allowed me six summers at school instead of the normal five.

I was keeping wicket as well as batting in those days, and there was close competition for the keeping position. I was selected for what was considered a slightly better keeping style and nothing to do with my batting.

I could bowl a bit, too, and was to fill this role in house matches; wicket-keepers seemed to grow on trees while fast bowlers were scarce. Wicket-keeping went by the board when my bowling was successful for the house.

I was given my 1st XI colours on the same day as my elder brother, John, as good a fast bowler as you would ever want to see. He would have played in the Lord's school games but for a self-imposed notion that neither batting nor fielding were up his street.

Batting instruction in those days was based on firm but simple slogans. Watch the ball, keep your head still, put your foot to the pitch of the ball. Bert Robinson, once of Northampton Cricket Club, would bowl tirelessly at us in the nets, and was never other than helpful and encouraging.

The other instructor was I. A. W. Gilliat, a fine cricketer in his own right, and a brilliant psychologist. By turns he would take each of the batsmen aside and assure him that his last dismissal was unavoidable, that the school never had such a good player in years, and that the boy would certainly get a packet of runs in the next match. The mind is delightfully straightforward at that age, so each of his batsmen, with the same story and belief in his head, would do exactly as 'Ivor' had told them.

We all made runs, time and time again, in fantastically quick time. Club sides set us to score 70, 80, 90, 100 an hour, and we always got them with minutes to spare. Two runs a minute became the accepted run rate to set our near-hypnotised batsmen, and still we won those declaration games.

Three of that side played at Lord's in the school games with a little but no great distinction. By this time, hundreds had become more frequent. I was playing on beautiful batting wickets among boys of my own age with good umpiring, and enough time to play proper innings. We were playing under ideal conditions from the ages of 14–18, a fact which played a large part in getting me into exalted cricketing ranks a few years later.

Playing on such good wickets has helped generations of Cambridge University cricketers to go on and play successfully for England.

Between school and Cambridge, I spent two years in the Army, and had the

*Ted Dexter with his parents in Barbados*

best part of two cricket seasons in Malaya. The local State clubs were very generous to the British Army players, and invited them to play whenever they could.

I hardly made a run in my first season out there. Whether the different light or the matting wickets were the trouble, I do not know, but I came good twelve months later and by making some runs I was able to repay the Negri Sembilan selectors for continuing to play me the previous year, when my performances hardly merited it.

To revert momentarily to my bowling career, I had bowled both off cutters and swingers at Radley, and had reasonable success. It was not the last time that I was to head both the batting and bowling averages.

It was in Malaya that the off cutters practically disappeared from my repertoire. We played a game on a matting wicket, and I was soon asked to bowl cutters by my captain. The first ball was a full toss, and so was the second, the third, fourth and fifth—finally a whole over of full tosses.

I was too frightened to try the same again next over. I decided to bowl as fast as I could and make sure that the ball pitched somewhere on the wicket, and never mind the length. My first few seemed genuinely quick, and the sensation of speed was most enjoyable. It was only at the tea interval that we discovered the pitch was two yards short, accounting for both the full tosses and my impressive pace.

I have hardly tried to bowl an off cutter since, but I have tried to develop the ability to swing the ball both ways, which is by no means as common as bowlers would have you believe.

National Service passed by without a game of very serious cricket, and it was in a very light hearted, demob-happy vein that I played in the Freshmen's trial games at Fenners. No thoughts of playing for the University had ever entered my head. I played for the fun of it, and nothing else.

I remember Steve Wheatley bowling me out time and time again in the nets, but I was entirely unworried. It may well be a pity I cannot take the game quite so light-heartedly now, but playing for enjoyment is still a big element in my cricket.

I made runs in those trial games, and hit the ball hard in every match. I hit my old friend Michael James a couple of times into the tennis courts, which was enough to catch Mike Melluish's eye as the captain-elect for that year. I found time to bowl fast at him one evening in the nets when the light was failing. I knocked his middle stump into the back of the net, whereupon he walked up to ask me to play for the University in the first three matches, against Surrey, Yorkshire and Lancashire.

Now I really felt way out of my depth. Loader, Trueman and Statham within ten days of starting first-class cricket were a bit of a handful.

Loader got me started with a duck, a well-pitched yorker that was removing the off stump while I was still flourishing the bat on my back swing—it was more like a golf back swing than the orthodox cricket 'pick up'—but I was as much a golfer as a cricketer in those days.

I was nervous as a kitten walking out for the second innings.

I hardly heard Robin O'Brien when he mumbled something about 'one off the mark' from Jim Laker. I gritted my teeth and hit the first ball, a long hop, as hard as I could to long leg. Thank goodness there was a fielder there, who made it just the single that Jim Laker was prepared to give me to save me from a pair on my first appearance.

*Peter Loader got me started with a duck*

It was then explained to me that 'one off the mark' was meant to be *one* and not *four*! I made three noughts and three forties in those games, and never lost my place in the University side for the next three years.

How lucky can you get? No young player on a ground staff could possibly get a regular place in a county side for that length of time, however promising his first efforts might be. But I was able to play all the best bowlers in England on batsmen's wickets for as long as I could stay there.

Two hours against Statham, Hilton and Greenhough in a match taught me twice as much as I could have learned in any amount of hours under a coach in county nets. And having no worries about losing my place in the side made batting twice as easy for me as for a young county player.

I thought I had given Mike Melluish convincing proof of my bowling ability, but it was obviously not that which decided him to have me in his side. I don't think he ever asked me to bowl a ball, and it was Gami Goonesena, the next year's captain, who gave me a bit of a chance.

I got him a few wickets at probably an astronomical cost, but it was my first opportunity to bowl at first-class batsmen. I remember my victims included Lowson and Cowdrey, so I was quite happy with my first efforts.

*Early days at Cambridge. 'Frank Lowson was one of my first victims'*

*Cambridge v. Lancashire. A bit of the golfer about this stroke, but it is not a bad cricket shot either*

Meanwhile, batting was becoming that much harder. I had been a strong off side and straight driver, but had very little else in the way of shots. The bowlers soon got fed up with bowling to my strength, and started bowling at my legs. This was something quite new to me and I started practising for hours trying to improve my leg side play. I succeeded and was well pleased with myself, until I found that all my good off side shots were gone.

I feel that a good coach could have put me right very quickly, but nobody who watched could put their finger on the trouble. Unconsciously, I started opening the face of the bat to try to steer the ball away on the off side. Leg side play became worse, off side play was no better, and that was the unhappy form I was in when called to Australia to join the M.C.C. in 1958.

I hardly made a run for them in the middle, and was no better in the nets. Fred Brown helped as much as he could. Jim Laker tried to get me going better, but all to no avail. Perhaps I was very stupid, but nothing they said could get me right.

But at last came a happy day—John Mortimer was bowling in the nets, and after one of my many mistimed shots, he asked me why I kept the face of the bat open. I said it wasn't open, but just straight up the wicket. He assured me

13

that whatever I thought I was doing didn't alter the fact that the blade was open and should be shut.

It was not till nets at Christchurch in New Zealand that the penny dropped. I spent half an hour belting the ball as hard as I knew straight back at the bowlers and with each well-timed shot, I knew that I was out of trouble, at least for a time.

The next day I made my first hundred for England.

Back in England in 1959, I played nearly a full season for Sussex and was given two chances of playing against India. In the Tests I made one fifty only and a couple of low scores. Slightly improved bowling and fielding got me on the trip to the West Indies with the M.C.C.

The summer with Sussex was memorable for playing under Robin Marlar. He was most sympathetic towards my efforts to learn the first-class game. He was always encouraging me to play naturally and to let things come with experience. Many low scores were interspersed with the odd good innings. A quick hundred against Worcester at Dudley, a hundred against Lancashire at Old Trafford were the highlights, but my showing in the Test Matches made me realize I had a lot to learn about taking a proper place in an England side.

Good things came early in the West Indies. Garfield Sobers dropped a caught and bowled when I was only twenty and that was the break I wanted. That mistake cost the West Indies another hundred and twenty runs.

I made runs quite consistently through the series and felt for the first time that I could bat competently against world-class bowling. Only two hundreds, but a lot of scores between forty and seventy showed that I had a lot to learn about building a large total. This takes a lot of experience for most people. At the start of an innings you must curb a few scoring shots that could get you out. Then as you get twenty and thirty you blossom naturally into playing more strokes and scoring quicker. The problem is to know when to stop. At some stage you must realize that you are playing as well as you can without giving the bowlers any more chance of getting you out. The temptation is always there to have a go, to try something new, and it usually ends in disaster.

The best batsmen reach this 'top gear' batting quickly in an innings, and can control themselves enough not to slip into overdrive. I used to find top gear almost too easily and be unable to keep myself in that groove for long enough.

I played most of the Tests against South Africa in England without doing anything very spectacular, but it was not a high scoring series, with conditions helping the South African bowlers almost every time England batted.

I had a successful county season, and made more than one bowler's mouth open with the odd shot I had learned from those fabulous West Indian batsmen.

No overseas tour that winter, a little time spent in the office, and a very nice few months spent at home without packing and unpacking, without farewells and reunions with my wife every few days.

The Australians came to England and retained the Ashes. After being bowled out at Birmingham on a wet wicket, England were struggling not to get beaten. I batted most of one day in the second innings for 180. I felt that it had been a defensive sort of innings, and yet the newspapers called it an innings full of good strokes.

I thought back to the Fourth Test against the West Indies where I had made a hundred in similar circumstances. Another penny dropped and I realized I could score quite quickly enough for the side, and even for the spectators, without having always to force the pace.

*Stumped Grout bowled Simpson 180—Birmingham 1961*

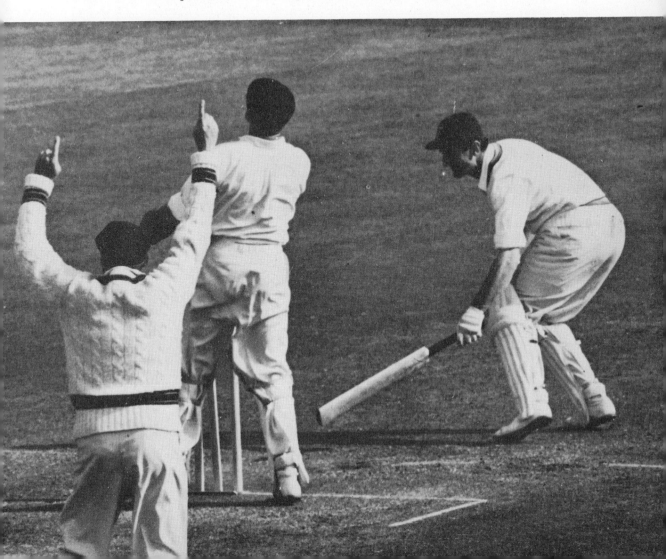

*Dexter the Golfer. Taking a practice swing before the Open Foursomes at Sunningdale, watched by his partner Peter Butler, the Harborne (Birmingham) professional*

It has been a hard lesson to learn, but watching Vijay Manjrekar throughout five Test Matches in India during the winter of 1961–2 was instructive, to say the least. He never hurried, never lost patience, was happy with ones and twos as long as they came regularly. He had great control in all his shots and though he was hardly a match-winning batsman, the situations never called for any heroics and his aggregate in the early Tests was very impressive.

I learned enough from him to make my first double century against Pakistan at Karachi. By no means a great innings, but I had achieved something I had set my heart on a couple of years before.

The series against Pakistan in England was not the scene for amassing large scores. I enjoyed every innings far too much to want to control myself to that 'top gear', but I hope the time will come when these hard learned lessons will bear fruit in some high scores which will help England to win matches and not just to draw.

16

One big psychological barrier that I have had to get over is the feeling that, however good you are—you can always get one very good ball that will get you out. This is, I suppose, one of the great merits of cricket—the chance factor that keeps every player from becoming over-confident, even keeps him humble.

Until I convinced myself that I might be good enough to go on scoring runs consistently over a period of time, only then could I bat sensibly and well from the beginning of an innings and concentrate properly from the first ball bowled. I have now played against a lot of very good bowlers and found that I can match skills with them without hesitating to build an innings from the start. If I get that very good ball, I may have learned something from it, and I know I may not get another one for some time.

For a long time, I was anxious to get runs on the board before I had settled down or felt the pace of the wicket, purely because of this fear of getting out early. I wanted to get some runs before the 'get out' ball.

It took time and experience before I could think my way through an innings from first to last, having been in control all the time. Only then did I know the full satisfaction of batting.

I used to play innings that satisfied me pretty well at the time. I might make a quick hundred with shots made spontaneously—a sort of reflex action rather than the result of a thought process. But I don't play much that way any more. I know the sort of shot to play to a particular bowler, and when the right ball comes along the right shot meets it. I know the sort of shots I am not going to play on perhaps a very slow wicket or against a certain bowler.

My other thoughts when batting are on getting the right blend of concentration and relaxation. Relaxation is as important in batting as it is for a runner or a pianist. Sometimes I tell myself 'Relax, relax', and then get worried that by relaxing I shall lose concentration, and do something slack and get out. And once out there is no coming back—that is the one harsh fact that the batsman must live with.

No other game is quite like cricket in this respect. There are three vital factors in batting—relaxation, concentration and the fear of getting out. Relaxation seldom comes naturally to a thoughtful batsman. But once a batsman has a hundred on the board, fear of getting out is no longer present in his mind, relaxation has become natural, and concentration has become a habit.

The great art must be to accept full responsibility for one's stay at the wicket, but somehow to get rid of the fear of getting out. Many great players have managed to do this by the very strength of their own characters. They seem to stand slightly aloof from the game. Bradman knew himself to be so good that he could concentrate on batsmanship without fear of getting out.

Hammond had a terrific presence when he walked on to the field. Compton achieved his freedom in batting in perhaps a slightly different way—more easy-going and debonair. They all had the ability to stand slightly aside from the main cares of the game.

Fear of playing one bad shot which gets you out can inhibit you completely and cut out all your other shots, even the safe ones. Until a few runs click up on the board, I find that things don't harmonize properly. Concentration without relaxation can curb every shot you ever knew. If you relax at the expense of concentration, you do something airy-fairy; if you are frightened of getting out you probably do nothing at all.

Mind you, a bowler does not always bowl the same ball by any means. Sometimes he bowls a sequence of balls which suit the batsman perfectly. The

*Tom Graveney. A study in poise, balance and concentration*

score rises quickly and safely, but when the bowler bowls his best, you cannot attempt to knock him off his length or you get into trouble. You must just wait for the first opportunity to score and then you may get the upper hand. If you miss that one, you really are in danger, and the bowler is that much more encouraged.

One interesting point about batting is the effect that the batsman at one end can have on the other. I probably play more shots early in an innings than most people, and this can affect a player who has been going steadily along—with the emphasis on 'steadily'.

With batsmen who are capable of batting more freely, it releases them, particularly when I am captain, and they think, 'What's all right for him is all right for me!' Very often the steady player starts to outscore me because I have allowed them to think that it is not the end of the world if they get out.

On the other hand, you get the chap who is genuinely limited in strokes. I join him at the wicket, and begin using quite a wide repertoire. With a young player, he may feel he is being made to look a bit silly, and must do something about it. He starts trying to do rather more than he can and promptly gets out.

My last words of advice on batting are very simple, but often very hard to put into practice. Don't move until the ball is in the air. It seems only sensible that you must see where the ball is going before trying to play it and yet the majority of players move before the ball is bowled.

Make certain of scoring off bad balls. Nothing encourages a bowler so much as bowling badly and not getting punished for it. He becomes encouraged and may even start believing he can get you out!

Phil Mead 'never encouraged bowlers' and made over 50,000 runs, so it may be sensible to follow his advice. It is easy to try to hit the bad ball too hard. I remember trying to hit a leg spinner outside the leg stump for four. Len Hutton was batting the other end, and I suspect there was a trace of a smile on his face when I missed the thing, and it turned and bowled me.

Sir Len accepted the fact that I knew I should have had my pads in the way. He didn't bother with technical advice, he merely said: 'Don't try to hit it so hard. As long as it goes for four, it doesn't matter how fast it goes over the line!'

On the other hand, I don't believe in pushing a ball for two when a bit more power would turn it into four. Runs are not so easy to come by that you can afford to miss half of them. Don't play at balls that are wide of the wicket unless you score off them. If you let them go by it is so much wasted effort on the part of the bowler, and you can never get out by letting them alone. You

*Peter May and Colin Cowdrey come in during their marathon innings against the West Indies*

should guard the wicket with your pads in case a freak ball which you have left alone bowls you.

There is a classic story of the newspaper report which said that a batsman was bowled by a ball which he should have left alone!

Finally, learn by watching good players. Copy their rhythm, stance, anything you like, and it will usually be for the good.

I remember watching May and Cowdrey on television during their record-breaking stand at Birmingham against the West Indies. I will swear I was a better batsman for a week after that, having a clear picture of them both in action in my mind's eye.

Those are only two of the batsmen and bowlers whom I have watched, read about and tried to copy. I want to tell you my impressions of many other great players and how they have affected my own game.

20

## Chapter 2

# TIPS FROM THE TOP

You can read and learn the basic strokes of batting from any coaching manual, the best, most thoughtfully produced being the new edition of the M.C.C. coaching book. I am not plugging this manual just because it has a photograph of me as its frontispiece! I recommend it as the result of much thought and hard work by people who are passionately interested in the game of cricket. They want all newcomers to be able to pick up a grounding of the game through simple written instruction backed by the best photographs available.

I often read the old edition of the M.C.C. coaching book and seldom put it down without finding my memory refreshed about some basically simple but vital part of the game.

It is not the basic strokes or rules that concern this chapter, but the application of them in high-class cricket.

I invite you to come with me and bat against some of the finest bowlers in the world, and I shall try to give you a running commentary with advice on how to play various types of bowling.

This sounds rather like the opening lines of a 'Sportsview' film while you prepare yourself to be taken down the St Moritz bobsleigh run or round the track at Silverstone in Stirling Moss's racing car.

I hope my commentary won't be so physically disturbing as most people find these photographic joy rides, although it might be even more frightening for the audience to see Wesley Hall, the great West Indian fast bowler, running up to bowl from way back in the middle screen distance, and to share the batsman's feelings throughout.

I walked out to bat against 'big Wes' for the first time when playing for Cambridge at Fenners when the West Indians last toured in England. At that time he was only a youngster and many people, including some of the other touring players, considered him lucky to have been invited to make the trip.

He was a wonderfully athletic, loose-limbed man who bowled off a fifteen-yard run and was recognized to be quite quick if conditions suited him. The wicket at Fenners has never suited any type of bowling particularly, and has made more than one fast bowler look pretty ordinary. I batted against Wes only in the second innings when the result of the match was already certain to be a draw. In those circumstances I felt that I could enjoy myself with some all-out aggression. I remember hitting a short ball from Wes over cover's head for four and being rather surprised at the shot after I had made it.

I hit him for one or two more fours without too much strain. I thought no more of Wesley Hall until we were due to face him in the First Test Match at Barbados in 1959. Remembering his bowling at Fenners, but having read between times of his fast bowling achievements in the West Indies and in India, I inquired of that great Barbados cricketer Denis Atkinson: 'How quick is Wes these days compared with Trueman and Statham?'

I remember his answer vividly as he spoke in that charming Barbados accent: 'No, no,' he said, 'Wes has got plenty of pace, plenty of pace.' He did not refer specifically to Fred or Brian, but he obviously meant that Wes was something out of the ordinary.

I remember even more vividly watching him run on to the field at the start of the Test Match, vying with Chester Watson to perform the most athletic warming up exercises, not that we Englishmen felt the need of such warming up under those kindly hot blue skies.

Wes was to bowl the first ball and marked out the longest run I had ever seen used by a bowler. Now all was set for the first show of pace, but at this vital moment, the umpire, looking at his watch, intervened, because it was still a minute before starting time. A hush descended on the whole ground as the batsman (was it Cowdrey or Pullar?) waited patiently, like a tethered goat awaiting the approaching tiger.

Big Wes literally pawed at the ground, waiting for the signal that would unleash weeks of fitness and training in a flash of co-ordinated effort. It was as though a space missile count-down had been delayed a minute on the stroke of zero with all the world waiting for lift-off. At last, after what seemed an ever-lasting minute, the umpire called play.

Wes broke into a smooth run now accelerating into a real sprint. As he gathered speed so the crowd of some thousands of local cricket fans started to

*Colin Cowdrey turns one from Chester Watson away to leg for 4*

23

roar in appreciation, spurring on their great bowler and at the same time giving the waiting batsman quite a lot more to think about.

Dependent on the situation of the game, this roar, which would rise to a crescendo as the ball was delivered, accompanied ball after ball, over after over, from the local hero. Certainly the first ball of the day was always a special moment when all voices were raised keeping time and company with the rhythmic run of the bowler. The first ball of the First Test Match had to be heard as well as seen to be believed.

As he neared the wicket both arms reached heavenward as arms, body and legs were gathered for the final assault.

The ball flew out of his hand faster than one could easily believe and hit the bat only a split second later with a terrific crack.

I have never been so thankful that I was not an opening batsman. I now knew the meaning of Denis Atkinson's simple phrase 'plenty of pace', and prepared to gear up the speed of my own batting to the speed of this great bowler.

England batted well that day and it was not until the second day that I had to walk to the wicket. A whole day and a night and part of another day I had spent in wondering whether I had the ability or technique to deal with Wesley Hall's thunderbolts. Now the moment had come and I was to be put to the test.

Fortunately I had had the privilege of watching Clyde Walcott play at Fenners only a season previously. Colin Smith was bowling very fast that year and I watched Clyde very carefully to see how he went about playing Colin on a good wicket. His first movement was always back on the stumps with his right foot while facing straight up the wicket. He was in position to hook short balls and yet had the strength and timing to drive the half volley off the back foot. Dangerous tactics on a wicket helping the fast bowler to move the ball off the wicket, but ideal for stroke play at Fenners or Barbados, which rank as two of the easiest wickets in the world for batsmen.

I remembered Clyde's tactics as I walked into the glare of that ideal little cricket ground in Bridgetown and resolved to use similar tactics but with one or two variations of my own.

After what I felt was only a preliminary skirmish against the spinners, I was faced by Wesley Hall himself. I played back automatically but came forward into the first ball as I saw that it was full length.

A sweet click and the ball was well timed, running where a mid-off might have been but wasn't, and I had scored four. The next ball was short, but I was already on the back foot, so I had time to play high and defensively and the ball dropped dead at my feet. It was a wonderful moment knowing that I

*Studied defence against Wes Hall in Kingston*

25

*Ramadhin*

could compete successfully with this great bowler, and largely because of some fairly simple observation a couple of years previously.

Ramadhin had also played at Cambridge on the West Indian tour of England and I still have the photograph of my dismissal 'lbw b Ramadhin'.

He must be the most difficult bowler in the world to play for the first time. He ambles a few paces to the wicket and, with a quick, hurried swing of the arm, appears to bowl a leg break. The next moment it hits the pitch and turns sharply from the off and you wonder whether your eyes are focusing properly.

26

Gamini Goonesena, our captain that year at Cambridge, implored all the batsmen to play Ram as an off spinner and hope to miss the leg spinner if it turned the other way. He played admirably himself and helped me to scramble a few runs against Ram when I batted with him. I probably played and missed a dozen times, but playing for the off break kept my wicket intact.

It was only when I became more adventurous and tried to read which way the ball would turn that I caused my own downfall.

I got on the back foot thinking to square cut what I was determined must be a leg break, but it was the same old deception and the umpire had no doubts about raising his finger as the ball came back from the off to hit my pads.

That was the last I saw of Ramadhin until Barbados in 1959.

The light was beautifully bright with magnificent flat cream walls for sight-screens against which the flight and spin of the ball are precisely and easily judged. Ramadhin ran in for his first ball to me and I steeled myself to play for the off break regardless. To my amazement he bowled me an off break, it looked like one, behaved like one from delivery to impact. Another and another, each a palpable off break and no optical illusions.

The following over he bowled me a leg break. This was the testing moment. Was I about to be deceived again? A split second and I was out of my misery— it was a leg break turning comfortably away from the wicket and Ramadhin never got me out again. He probably will do before he finishes his long and brilliant career, but for a few months in sunshine and on good wickets, I was able to keep the upper hand. It may have been the grey English skies and frequently bad backgrounds that made him such a scourge to England's batsmen on his two touring visits to this country.

Slow bowling of his type needs a relaxed and sensitive batting approach, a kinship with the flight and spin of the ball whose curve and bounce can be judged soon after it is in the air. Frankie Worrell has this gift above all other players I have watched, very relaxed but watchful, working with the spin of the ball to his own advantage.

Fast bowling requires quick decisive movement, keyed up to the pace of the bowler. Not too much movement of the bat will increase the safety factor, so that the extra fast ball does not break through an only partially completed stroke.

Garfield Sobers, in my opinion the greatest cricketer the world has ever produced, is an unusual type of bowler to play against. He can bowl fast, medium pace cutters, swing, and every known form of left arm slow bowling. I first played him at Cambridge when he bowled left arm orthodox spin, turning from leg. He bowled rather too fast to turn the ball much, but was accurate and had a very well disguised quicker ball.

In the West Indies he had discarded the orthodox for wrist spin bowling and was bowling 'chinamen' and googlies, left arm over the wicket.

It was a blessing to play against him first at Barbados where getting the ball to turn is a near impossibility. Whether 'chinaman' or googly, the ball is sure to carry straight on after it hits the ground and no great technique is required— just the ability to pick the length of the ball, hit the bad ones and either play defensively or allow the good ones to go by.

The danger ball was not always the good length ball that was going to hit the wicket. Garfield got quite a few players out trying to pull the ball dropped short on the leg stump. A correct enough shot to the chinaman, but the googly

*O'Neill pulls Sobers off the leg stump to the boundary in the third Test at Brisbane, 1960. But Sobers had the final say—he bowled O'Neill for 71*

would occasionally bounce higher and turn from leg—the intended pull would get the ball high on the outer edge of the bat, and 'caught at wicket' or 'caught and bowled' would be written in the score book. Garfield has since had considerable success against Australia, bowling his faster stuff, and it will be interesting to see which style he uses in England in 1963.

I never quite understood why the South Africans were not more successful on their tour of England in 1960.

They had some experienced batsmen and three very fine bowlers of difficult types in Adcock, Tayfield and Trevor Goddard. They must have been disappointed and unsettled when their other pace bowler Griffin was pushed out of the firing line, but they are tough, dedicated cricketers who would not let that sort of thing get them down easily. Their batsmen met Statham and Trueman in one of their very best years, but after they had bowled them out once, some of the batsmen started to try to use different styles of batting. The English press were adamant that they should play forward more to counteract the swing of Trueman and the sharp movement off the wicket of Statham. This is all very well for English players who have been brought up on such principles, but not much help to established players who have their own methods which have proved successful on many other occasions.

The South Africans soon played a match where the wicket was as good and flat as their own at home. Yet again they were bowled out because they adopted techniques quite foreign to them, when their own original styles would have been perfectly sound and successful.

What a fine tour Adcock had that summer. He was chosen as one of the Cricketers of the Year and was certainly a great bowler for those few months. He had had trouble with injuries throughout his career, but that summer in England he never left the field or missed a match through injury. He bowled every inch of his great height, about $6\frac{1}{2}$ feet.

Some critics said he did not use enough body, but they should have batted against him to realize that his upright whirlwind arm action made up for any other shortcomings.

The ball bounced high, hitting the bat near the splice or one's thigh if the bat did not get there in time. He moved the ball very sharply off the wicket, particularly into the right-hand batsmen. Often he was just plain awkward to play, though not too difficult from the point of view of his getting your wicket. For the first few Test Matches he bowled anyone else's normal good length but with his extra bounce he seldom hit the wicket.

Almost all his victims were caught—wickets came slowly but at very little cost, because the ball was never up for the drive and deflections only got one run.

*Jackie McGlew in action against the Duke of Norfolk's XI at Arundel. Behind the stumps is Godfrey Evans, with Roy Marshall in the covers*

Realizing that he was beating the bat very often without getting a wicket, he started to bowl more at the wicket in the later matches. His victims came either more quickly or not at all, and therefore they cost him a few more runs per wicket. He was certainly a more dangerous bowler in his latter style, but not nearly so awkward to play against.

I suppose he should have bowled at the wicket with the new ball and at new batsmen, and then reverted to that shorter lifting length when the ball became older and the batsmen more settled, which after all is a pretty old maxim of fast bowling.

Hugh Tayfield was supposedly past his best on that last South African tour in England, and indeed he probably did not bowl as consistently well as in previous years. However, when he was having an on-day, he was as dangerous as ever.

I remember he bowled far below his best at Manchester and I hit him for a few fours and a couple of sixes. The critics asked why in the world I had not done that before in earlier Test Matches. The simple answer was that he bowled infinitely better on those other occasions and such aggression would have probably got me out.

His line was most unusual. His front foot would make a big swivel mark right in front of the stumps, and his hand came over at least leg stump or even more to leg. A straight ball pitching middle would hit the off stump and therefore normal rules of playing an off spinner to leg with the spin did not apply.

*Tayfield. His front foot coming down right in front of the stumps and his arm over leg stump*

His field was set with only four on the leg side and two of those in catching positions. Very often two silly mid-ons, one saving the single at square leg and the fourth halfway to the boundary behind the silly mid-ons.

After Tayfield bowled he would come to a dead stop poised as another close fielder in front of the wicket. A slip and four men in the covers completed his field with only a rather deep mid-off being out of the ordinary.

The great temptation was always to want runs in that big open space to mid wicket, but this was Tayfield's trap.

He spun only the occasional ball, so shots to mid wicket were often played across the ball with no spin to lessen the risk.

Those two silly mid-ons were ready to catch even the hardest hits in the air, and that halfway fielder could still cut off all but the cleanest drives. He was

31

tremendously accurate, and his field placing depended on his ability to bowl immaculately straight at the wicket.

For a while no ball would turn and I would start thinking that I should play him for runs on the off side.

Then I would become over ambitious in that area, and it only needed one ball to turn a little and Hughie had another victim.

Even Denis Compton admits that he never quite knew how to go about dealing with Hughie. He went down the wicket, stayed at home, tried his famous sweep, but never gained any great advantage against a bowler who really had something out of the ordinary.

Trevor Goddard has gone through two phases in his bowling career due to the limiting only recently of the leg side fielders to five, with only two of these behind the wicket.

Before the leg side limitation Trevor would bowl purely defensively, swing-

*Tayfield snaps up a low catch off his own bowling to dismiss Denis Compton at Johannesburg*

ing the ball into the right-hand batsman's legs with six fielders on the leg side. No great threat to the batsman unless he tried to score runs, but every defensive over Trevor bowled brought the new ball nearer for Heine and Adcock to launch another speed attack. After the introduction of the leg side limitation, and incidentally the loss of Heine from the South African bowling strength, Goddard had to attack the stumps more, and many think he became a better bowler as a result.

The art of playing these left arm over the wicket bowlers is not to follow the ball over on the off side. So many balls are just going across the wicket and through to the wicket-keeper. If the ball swings in and if you have not followed it over to the off side, then you are in a perfect position to play it as it comes back toward the wicket.

Alan Davidson must be the greatest contemporary left arm fast bowler, although I have recently seen a near replica of him called Jones playing for Glamorgan.

Davidson has all the gifts for a fast bowler—great strength and plenty of all-round cricket ability. Again I always try to stand my ground and be willing to see the ball sail past the off stump much of the time.

He cannot afford to bowl at the wicket once the shine has gone off the ball, because so many runs will come easily on the leg side. It is a great help to be a good cutter against this type of bowling—there is not much danger of dragging the ball on to your stumps, and you have plenty of opportunity to use the shot if you play it well.

You can read the score sheet at the end of any Australian match in which Davidson and Grout are both playing and more often than not you will read 'A. N. Other, c Grout b Davidson'. Much of the praise for these wickets must go to the bowler, but Wally Grout never lets a chance go begging to make this great partnership with Davidson.

Richie Benaud's name springs immediately to mind when one talks of Davidson and Grout.

They have been Test Match campaigners together throughout their careers. Richie is a fine leg break bowler and, like all bowlers of his type, he has his own little tricks which a batsman must get to know.

Richie can change suddenly from an all-out attacking bowler using his every change of pace and flight to bowl you out, to the steadiest defensive slow bowler imaginable! They say that he sometimes decides to deny a batsman a single run practically on pain of death to a fielder who does not play his part. This ability to attack and defend as a bowler, doing both things supremely well, makes Richie one of the all-time great bowlers.

33

I have not seen players use their feet with much success to Richie. He has a certain natural flight and dip, but never seems to bowl very slowly. I look for runs off Richie on the back foot, but therein lies considerable danger because I am quite sure that I am giving him a better chance of getting me out.

This bears out a rather more general theory of mine that against high-class bowling the safest way is to play forward and yet the most runs will come if you are a good back-foot player.

I hope this insight into actual conflict with these great bowlers has brought you nearer the Test Match scene, and that when they bowl again you may watch with renewed interest.

## Chapter 3

# IT'S NOT CRICKET

To admit that people have cheated at cricket, even a little, is much like suspecting the integrity of the lady who holds the scales of justice high above the Old Bailey. Perhaps that hallowed building should indeed be the place of trial for players who, by cheating, try to destroy that most English of sayings, 'It's not cricket'.

'It's not cricket', said more than one member of the English public on hearing of Hitler's advance into Poland, defying every assurance given to Neville Chamberlain.

'It's not cricket', said a spectator at Twickenham as the players had a stand-up fist fight to settle some small difference of opinion started in the depths of the scrum.

Public and spectator alike were not making small talk to their nearest neighbours by explaining that war and rugby were not cricket, but were condemning immoral and unfair behaviour in the most complete and final way known to the world. Are cricketers conscious of their responsibility when playing their own game?

One captain was batting with an older and more experienced member of his team who was taking strike at the time. The captain was amazed to see his team mate tickle one to the wicket-keeper, but make no attempt to walk out. The bowler appealed, the umpire raised his finger and the batsman retired sheepishly to the pavilion.

The captain followed suit without much delay and asked for an explanation of the other batsman's behaviour.

35

'It was such a faint tickle, captain, I thought I might be allowed to stay.'

'It's not cricket', said the captain, and he was right.

Strangely enough, of the various ways that it is possible to cheat at cricket, the act of not walking out when you know you should is probably the only one available to the batsman.

The situation crops up so often in every match, and it is this repetition that makes correct behaviour almost a necessity.

Umpires agree that a batsman's actions give them quite a lot of help in giving decisions. The wicket-keeper's actions will probably influence the umpire just as much. Most 'keepers will shout a whole-hearted appeal and barely bother to look at the umpire when they know they have taken a fair catch.

The story goes that George Duckworth would take the catch, be loud in his appeal, throw the ball high into the covers and sit down talking to first slip waiting for the next batsman to come in, never having given so much as a glance at the umpire to see whether he agreed with the Duckworth verdict.

I imagine he occasionally suffered the indignity of having to get up and take the next ball standing behind the same batsman as before, but it must have been a strong-willed umpire to say 'Not out' against such clear indications to the contrary.

I am sure that George Duckworth was less forthright on occasions when he was not so certain of having fairly dismissed the batsman. But there is no denying the opportunity given to some wicket-keepers to 'put on an act' in the middle of a warm afternoon's fielding, directing the umpire, more surely than by any conversation, to give the poor batsman out regardless of whether he did really touch the ball.

Wicket-keepers are certainly well placed to do a little cheating, standing so close to the central focus of the game. The base of the stumps, for instance, can be nudged with the nearest toe as the ball passes nearby.

Poor Gerry Alexander, the wicket-keeper for the West Indies in Australia, experienced a most unhappy moment of this kind in a Test at Melbourne. Wally Grout shaped to cut a ball from Valentine. The ball went through Gerry's legs, or between him and slip, as the batsman went for a run.

Meanwhile Gerry was standing with gloves open appealing to the umpires, showing them that the off bail was on the ground. The umpires had obviously watched the ball and not seen the bail fall, but in giving Grout 'not out' it was tantamount to saying that Gerry had knocked the bail off himself.

I saw a film of the incident over and over again, and there was no possibility of Gerry having touched that bail or the wicket, but the incident illustrates the vital position of the wicket-keeper in being so near to the wicket and to the

*Grout hesitantly completes the run, while the bewildered Gerry Alexander appeals to the umpires. The offending bail is nowhere in sight*

37

batsman.

Much the same thing happened in the England v. Australia Test Match at Melbourne in 1958–9, but this time the wicket-keeper was not involved. Fiery Fred Trueman bowled a fast short ball and Colin Macdonald pushed it away to fine leg, having played right back near his wicket to do so. As the ball was fielded and returned, it was seen that a bail was on the floor. Not only that, but there was a stud mark right up against the base of the stump. I suppose the umpires, not having actually seen the bail fall, were technically correct in giving Macdonald 'Not out', but Fred was not pleased at these technicalities I can assure you.

Macdonald certainly did not know what had happened, although he agreed later that it must have been his foot which disturbed the wicket.

He behaved quite admirably on another occasion in the Test Match at Adelaide. He had injured himself in the course of a very long innings and was using a runner. He played a shot and called for a run. The other batsman and the runner hesitated, but finally made the attempt. Mel McInnes the umpire made a mistake in going the wrong side of the wicket to make the run out decision, and though he saw the wicket broken, Macdonald's runner completed the run behind McInnes' back.

Everyone on the ground but the unfortunate umpire knew that the run had not been completed and Macdonald should be out. McInnes had no option but to say 'Not out' as he had not seen the whole action himself.

Macdonald had a good view, however, from the other end and got himself out purposely a couple of balls later.

It should be a point of honour with all batsmen to walk when they know they are out, without even looking at the umpire, but this system of 'honour' does lead to other difficulties.

Batsmen have been known to walk out for a catch at the wicket when every fielder would bet a month's wages that bat and ball never made contact.

It is none too charitable to suggest that on these occasions it is not always the batsman's judgment that is at fault but his courage. If fast bowlers are getting a bit dangerous, then a near miss can be translated into a snick by the irresolute batsman who then makes a bee-line for the pavilion before anyone can recall him. But this is only cheating his own side of a few runs perhaps, and he hardly deserves to have to stand trial at the Old Bailey, as should the more intentional cheat.

Manifestations of little courage are not always as obvious as this even to the fielding side. Fast bowlers on fast or uncertain wickets can put fear of some sort into the stoutest heart, even if it is only the fear of getting out, but even on a

*David Larter in full cry—a fearsome sight to any batsman*

good wicket the fast bowler can know how courageous his opponent is without ever bowling a dangerous ball. A movement backward before the ball is bowled will show a dislike of the short ball, and leave the batsman more vulnerable to the full-length delivery.

Some players shuffle and fall over to the off, wanting to be well inside the line of the short ball when it comes, while the worst and most obvious offenders back away to leg so that the only thing the ball can hit is wooden—either bat or wicket will do, and they don't care much which.

Lack of courage in bowling is not very obvious and may only be shown by a bowler not trying his best when things don't go right for him.

Fielding can demand a high degree of physical courage, particularly in the close catching positions. The close positions on the leg side, forward short leg and silly mid-on, are certainly the most vulnerable to direct and unavoidable blows. The only consolation for fielders in these positions is perhaps the survival of Arthur Milton after a terrific blow in the face in a Gentlemen v. Players game at Lord's.

Peter Richardson was batting, and was perhaps slightly deceived by the flight of a slow delivery so that he did not move a muscle while the ball was well on its way toward him. At the last split second he decided to sweep.

Arthur Milton was given no warning at all before the ball, hit sweetly on the meat of the bat, crashed into his nose and cheek at point blank range. He went down as if for ever, and yet was smoking a cigarette between quickly swelling lips only a couple of minutes later. The fact that he still fields in dangerous positions and catches as well as ever speaks volume for his courage.

It has been known that fielders in the deep, when presented with a high catch, make sure that they never quite get into the right position, and finally just fail to get a hand to the ball. By so doing they hope that the undiscerning eye will credit them with a good attempt to get to the ball, rather than damning their faint heart in never quite getting to it. This is known as 'running fast to get there last'.

Some people will catch well when the game is easy, but come the vital catch of the match and their nerve fails them. Unhappy thoughts, but they may help the spectator and player alike to assess character and courage on the field. But lack of courage is rather a large digression from actual cheating.

The fielder can cheat in various ways, but none more vital to the game than by unfairly claiming a doubtful catch.

Another system of 'honour bright' has grown in first-class cricket that the only person who really knows whether he has made a fair catch is the catcher himself. If the fielder in the slips says to the batsman, who may not have seen the catch taken, 'Yes, I caught it', then the batsman will, within the system, walk out without bothering the umpire.

This system works admirably most of the time, because often a fielder may be shielded from the view of both umpires, and they may have to judge 'Not out' a perfectly fair catch which they have not seen actually made.

Now both fielder and batsman can ruin the system by letting the slightest doubt mar his sincerity. A fielder claiming a fair catch when he is not certain, or a batsman waiting for the umpire's decision against the word of the fielder, can cause endless difficulty and discord between sides.

I do not believe that a catcher is entitled to think himself 100 per cent sure

*Arthur Milton right in the firing line at short leg—but this time the batsman failed to connect*

of having made a fair catch. A ball may come quick and low in the slips, a fielder, not quite alert, sticks down a hand and feels it go in with a smack. Surely it can feel just the same whether on the 'fly' or on the half-volley.

There have certainly been some most unhappy incidents in Test cricket over this one feature of the game. The much filmed catch at short leg by Kline off Colin Cowdrey's bat at Brisbane was one such when the fielder claimed a fair catch, and yet there seemed to be a reasonable doubt as to whether he was right. On this occasion Cowdrey doubted the catch, but walked out when assured by Kline that the catch was fair.

Another 'headline' catch decision decided the last series between the West Indies and Australia in the fourth Test Match at Adelaide.

With only one wicket needed for a West Indian victory, and with every West Indian fielder crowded round the bat, Mackay of Australia was desperately playing out time. Suddenly Mackay pushed forward, and Sobers, fielding almost at the end of the bat, threw the ball high in the air delighted at having taken the match winning catch. The fielders started to leave the field but the batsman

41

*High drama at Adelaide. Lindsay Kline playing Worrell, with Sobers literally inches from the bat. At the other end is Ken Mackay*

stood his ground. A despairing appeal to the umpire could really only bring one response. Such catches are only a fraction of a second in the air. Was it a bump ball? Did the ball touch the ground through the fielder's fingers? How can an umpire be absolutely certain of all these things, and, once put to the test, he must give the benefit of the doubt to the batsman.

On this occasion he said 'Not out' and the match was drawn. There is much to be said for umpires giving decisions on all occasions and doing away with the appeal altogether.

The batsman would still be entitled to walk out if he knew he were out. The umpire would give him 'Out' immediately and would probably still raise his finger, even to the retreating back of the batsman who left of his own accord. The absence of the appeal, however, would rob cricket of one of its more lively moments.

The concerted HOWZAT! of a fielding side can awaken the most dedicated sun worshipper, who comes to cricket matches to follow his favourite hobby. The bowler must be in the best position to do a bit of checking, though I often wonder whether a batsman would ever be found out if he used a bat just slightly broader than the regulation size!

Keith Miller and Freddie Trueman are well known for running their hands through well-greased hair, and then applying the same hand to the ball, no doubt providing a high gloss. But is this any worse than the old army method of 'spit and polish'? I spit on the ball, on my hands, and polish the ball through two or three pairs of flannels a season. (Thank goodness for man-made fibres, or it would be more like thirty!) Nobody has called me a cheat yet.

Nobody has ever called Keith or Freddie a cheat either and lived to tell the tale, but then hair cream is not specifically mentioned in the rules of cricket as 'aid to bowlers'.

*A typical Australian appeal. An exciting moment guaranteed to shake the drowsiest spectator*

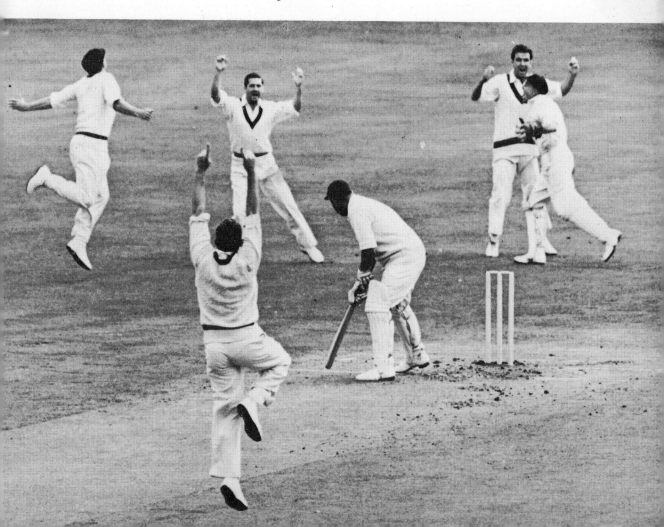

A word of warning here to those seam bowlers who may copy my 'spit and polish' methods. I used practically to lick the ball direct, and soon had raw gums for my pains. I now spit on my hands and keep my mouth clean, but it doesn't make white flannels any cheaper.

The name of 'seam bowler' rather than 'fast' or 'medium pace' has grown quite recently, and from reading books on cricket played between the wars, there seems little doubt that bowlers were not then so aware of the way a ball can pitch on the seam, grip the turf, and thereby change direction. Descriptions of good bowlers were more likely to read, 'he got a lot of work on the ball', rather than the modern description 'he gets a lot of movement off the seam'.

Particularly on English wickets, which are seldom very hard, the seam bowler can be very effective, as he can move the ball enough to take wickets, and yet bowl fast enough to keep the runs down.

The new ball particularly will grip on the seam, as each stitch is still fresh and standing out from the ball. After a few overs the stitches are pushed down flat, and mud gets between them, making the ball smoother and less help to the bowler.

Now a bowler is quite at liberty to try to clean the mud off the ball, but he is almost certain to raise the stitches again if he picks it out with a finger-nail. This is normally known as 'picking' the seam, and is not allowed within the rules of the game, but a few bowlers pick the stitches up until they resemble a saw edge.

With a little judicious practice at home, it is possible to pick the seam with a thumb-nail even while running up to bowl, and remain quite undetected by the umpires. Much more difficult to deceive are the viewers at home, getting a close-up view on their television screens, but I suppose all great artists can learn new tricks to suit a new medium!

Umpires are quite lenient normally, and I have not yet seen a bowler asked to produce the ball for inspection, but there must be a first time, and there may be a very red face or two when that moment comes.

The whole question of what you may and may not do to the ball once in play is complex, and no absolute code of behaviour has been evolved. Umpires allow the seam of the ball to be cleaned but not raised; they allow the ball to be polished with sweat, look slightly disapproving of spit, quite angry at grease from the hair, and would certainly take action at a tin of boot polish.

The ball can be rubbed in the dirt by a spin bowler in front of the umpire so that he can grip the ball better, but any further act would be considered as interfering with the natural state of the ball. There is a better case for damping and polishing the ball and thereby preserving it, than roughing the surface and thereby shortening its life.

In South Africa, however, there is a much more strict interpretation of these rules, and no licking, spitting, greasing or roughing the ball is tolerated.

In England this attitude would serve the game very well, and, though it would work against my particular type of bowling, I believe it would make for more attractive cricket. On the well-grassed outfields of the big grounds, the ball can remain smooth, and if damped and polished it becomes shiny. Medium pace bowlers can get a better swing all day, and are therefore more effective and economical than slow bowlers. Medium pace bowlers thus bowl continuously and reduce the tempo of the game drastically.

The South African attitude that the ball should be left in its normal state until a new one is taken would mean the ball getting rougher sooner, the medium pace bowler would get less help, and the slow bowlers would certainly bowl more, much to the added enjoyment of both players and the crowds.

Another situation arises that can provide a real headache for the umpires under the heading of fair and unfair play. When the batsmen go for a run, the fielder is entitled to get the ball and try to run one of them out. Often, the batsman will obstruct the fielders' clear view of the wicket and will purposely run between the thrower and the wicket, willing to take a crack on the head or in the back to avoid being run out.

No batsman has ever, to my knowledge, been given out in these circumstances for unfair play, but the umpire is severely tested, when batsman and fielder are trying to use the same ground, and collision or baulking of one or the other takes place. This sort of decision comes quite easily to the stewards of the course at Ascot, or at any other race meeting, and nowadays they have the mobile camera to help them in their findings. But the cricket umpire experiences the situation only very occasionally, and has no photographic evidence to help him.

It's a nice thought that umpires of the future may sit in front of a series of television screens, with 'photo finish' equipment at the ready, to help them in any decision they must make.

At the Oval during the fifth Test Match, in the last series against South Africa, Jackie McGlew was called for a pretty short single as the ball was played just to the side of the wicket, where he would be running. Brian Statham went for the ball as fast as he could and got it in his hand, but in so doing he crossed immediately in front of Jackie, who tripped over him.

Brian completed a brilliant and determined piece of fielding by throwing the wicket down, with Jackie scrambling for home. The umpires had to say 'Out', unless they considered that Jackie had been unfairly obstructed. Brian had obviously not obstructed intentionally, but all the fielders would willingly have had Jackie recalled to continue his innings. The umpires were asked whether this could be done, but they rightly agreed that their correct decision must stand.

As I see it, if the batsmen decide to take a run when the ball is somewhere near the wicket, they must accept the fact that the fielder has just as much right to be fielding the ball as the batsman has to be running.

The incident just described was rather more fair play than on another occasion at the Oval, when Ken Barrington played a shot and went for a run. As he raced for the far end he came face to face with the bowler, and they proceeded to do a side-stepping act, as we all do every day on crowded pavements, each going the same way.

Poor Ken was easily run out, and here I feel the umpires might have intervened on his behalf. Even though the final obstruction may not have been absolutely intentional, a bowler has plenty of time to give the batsman room to run, and should never get into this unfortunate position, unless fielding the ball himself. I have often felt like tripping the batsman on his way past after he has hit me for runs, but I have not succumbed to the temptation yet!

Peter May figured in another interesting situation when playing for Surrey in a county game. He played a fine shot in the air but saw one of the fielders take the catch rolling over. He started to walk away toward the pavilion thinking himself to be out. The catch had, in fact, been dropped, and as Peter walked out of his ground, the fielder returned the ball smartly to run him out. It must strike anyone as a pretty unfair way of getting someone out.

Perhaps the rules should give the umpires power to recall a batsman who gets out under these rather freak conditions, and I feel they could have intervened in this case, considering it unfair play.

I want to cover as many as possible of these minor anomalies in the game, and perhaps the rules may be varied slightly in the future to keep cricket pure as the driven snow. There is no point in allowing temptation to lie for years in the path of players who may finally be tempted to take advantage.

Bowlers sometimes kick the stumps down at their own end in the very act of bowling. The batsman is surely seriously distracted, and may well be bowled out, but the umpire has no power to recall him, unless he considers that the bowler distracted him purposely.

So much fuss is made about crowds walking behind the bowler's arm, absolute quiet and stillness being supposedly essential to the batsman, yet the bowler may kick the wicket over, grunt and say 'Sorry', all in the moment the ball leaves his hand, but then, without a pang of remorse, watch the poor

*Umpire Hugo Yarnold recalls Peter May to the crease after May had 'walked' thinking himself caught by Smith in the Surrey v. Sussex match last year*

batsman on his way back to the pavilion.

A bowler doing anything to distract the batsman, whether intentionally or otherwise, should be called for a 'No ball' by the umpire, and then temptation would be put away for ever.

Should fielders move their positions while the ball is being bowled, thus deceiving the batsman?

A lively first slip can sometimes be useful down the leg side, if he cares to move over once the ball starts in that direction. Some catches have been taken in this way, which must have been most spectacular at the time, but I feel that such play could easily be extended to every fielder, and then the game would

47

degenerate into a grotesque version of Grandma's Footsteps.

But we cannot surely perpetuate this wonderful old adage 'It's not cricket'—immortal words which have meant just as much in Calcutta, Hong Kong and Moscow as they have in the cricketing centres of London, Melbourne and Kingston, Jamaica—if we allow the show piece of the game, first-class cricket, to be conducted in even a vaguely underhand manner.

For this reason, if no other, cricket is the one game in which players must 'play the game', even when pushed to the limit of their patience by circumstance.

At the end of a five-day battle of wits and courage, there may come the moment when a player has to choose to play the game properly and lose, or play it only slightly unfairly and win. In any other game a player might 'play it hard' in that last resort, and look to critics to forgive him in the heat of the moment. He may indeed well be forgiven, but, please Heaven, never let that happen in cricket.

There have been attempts to sully the great name of cricket and play it to the necessities of the minute without regard for the game itself or its future. The bodyline tour in Australia was one such. How could England stop Bradman scoring, and thereby have a chance of winning? Not by fair means, because they had been tried by a number of bowlers and captains with conspicuously little success.

Fast bowlers and captain now conspired together to turn batting into a most hazardous occupation, persistently bowling to hit the batsman and not the wicket. Such bad feeling existed between players, and even between the countries, that Commonwealth ties were seriously threatened.

In 1958 Australia got their revenge with a battery of throwers purporting to bowl, dismissing the flower of England's batting with contemptuous ease. This was not cricket, and very little honour was reflected on either teams or administrators for the outcome of the tour, because England were very little less to blame in the throwing controversy than the Australians.

Don Bradman, Gubby Allen, Gerry Gomez, Jahanger Khan, Vijay Merchant, Geoff Chubb and Wally Hadlee—surely these fine cricketers and representatives of great cricketing countries can make sure that the game will be played to its highest traditions at the highest level. They, and all players, have it in their hands to keep the game worthy of that simple and most characteristic phrase of the English language: 'It's not cricket.'

*Chapter 4*

# MY CRICKETING ALPHABET

Attack really is very often the best form of defence both in batting, bowling and fielding. One brilliant attacking shot can ruin the best bowler's accuracy. One good catch taken by a close fielder, who may have little right to be standing so close, can turn the course of a match.

It is this change of the game by one stroke, or a bit of luck, that provides the game's greatest fascination.

Defensive play is part of the game of cricket, but it has become over-revered by captains and players as a general passport to success. Two hours' defensive bowling may achieve only what a fielder in an attacking position can do in a split second, leaving the game those two hours younger and that much nearer a result.

Attacking players are sometimes rather frowned upon in first-class cricket. Someone who gets bowled having a full-blooded drive at the ball, probably looks sillier than another who gets out pushing defensively. The first seems to have been bowled through his own fault while the second may claim that it must have been a very good one to beat his studied defence!

Spectators and players alike prefer attacking cricket, and it is up to schools, coaches and captains all round the country, in every grade of cricket, to instil the idea of attack into all cricketers.

*Bouncers or bumpers* have been much discussed in the past year. There have been many accidents, and one feels that it is only a matter of time before a fatal accident to a well-known cricketer really makes bowlers think about aiming these short balls at the head.

49

Attack 1. *Dexter hits out—this time to be caught by Burki off Intikhab*

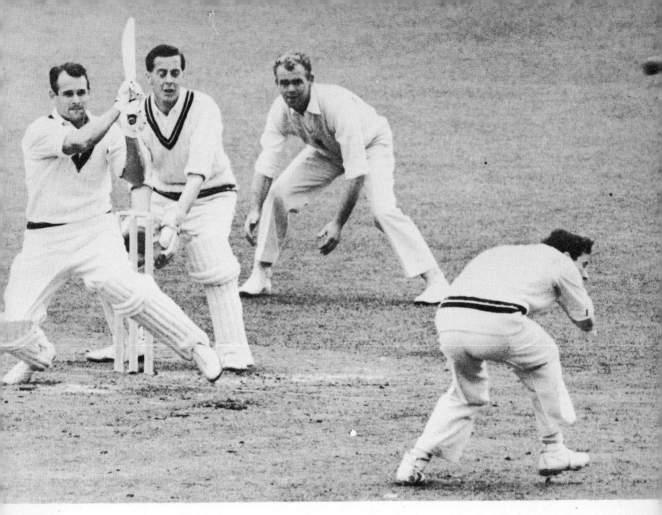

Attack 2. *O'Neill scatters the close field*

The best fast bowlers bowl the bouncer only against a batsman who plays forward before judging the length of the ball. These players deserve the warning bouncer perhaps, but continual use of this type of ball is both dangerous and unnecessary.

The greatest bumper warfare was waged in the 'bodyline series' under Jardine in Australia. There was no restriction on the number of fielders on the leg side at that time, so players had either to avoid the bouncer if they could, or risk getting out by trying to hook. The England v. West Indies series in 1960 was marred in many ways by the continual bowling of bouncers. The bowlers had a very difficult job on their hands trying to get wickets on those beautiful strips of turf, but I do not believe that bouncers, though often effective, are the correct and ethical way of going about the task.

51

Bouncers. *West Indies opener Easton McMorris ducks this one from Fiery Fred*

*Confidence* is important enough in any competitive sport, but surely never more so than in cricket.

Watch a batsman walk out to bat with some runs already on the scoreboard and there is something unmistakable about his gait. Something very different from the batsman who has had a lot of low scores recently, and can hardly imagine where his next run will come from.

It is all a matter of confidence, and it affects not only the player himself, but the other batsman with him, and even the bowlers and fielders. You can often see a batsman in good form getting all sorts of bad balls even from good bowlers. His confidence has risen above theirs and they wonder where on earth to bowl at all instead of how to bowl him out.

Watch a slip fielder who has already caught two easy catches make the next sharp chance look as easy as the first two. Relaxed and confident he will pick the ball out of the air as though by magic. Then watch the poor unfortunate short leg who has grassed an easy one—he may have been moved to a position where a catch is unlikely and yet the ball will often seem to follow a bad fielder to add to his discomfort. Tense hands and over eager movements will see our erstwhile short leg drop another dolly catch.

Confidence is all important and it is a great part of a captain's work to bolster the confidence of every player, but particularly of those who are having a bad run.

*Dedication* to the game is almost a must. Cricket takes such a long time to play, particularly Test cricket, that there is the opportunity to get side-tracked into other activities which break your concentration. Some players appear to be able to stand apart from the game and play it light-heartedly and successfully at the same time. I think this is really a mannerism and that success comes only

Energy 1. *Energy comes from fitness and you have to be fit to move like this. John Murray brings off a superb 'save'*

to those who have the game very near their heart and who put every ounce of effort into it all the time. Bowlers, particularly, must have almost a sense of vocation towards their trade, and the very best of them certainly talk in a dedicated way about their work.

*Energy* comes from fitness, and fitness comes from plenty of exercise and plenty of sleep. If you have these two in sufficient doses, in my team you can please yourself just how you acquire them. Perhaps we should include smoking among permissible entertainments, but I cannot believe that smoke in the lungs rather than clear air can help anyone's wind and stamina.

Batting demands its own fitness. It demands long periods of concentration, and if a batsman becomes tired his concentration will weaken at the same time.

I remember becoming quite exhausted from the heat during an innings at Port of Spain, Trinidad. I got cramp and had to take salt to counteract it.

Energy 2. *Same match—same wicketkeeper*

Fielding. *Dexter drives Mackay. The field is alert and watchful*

Somehow the thread of the innings was lost and I was soon out playing a half-hearted and ill-considered shot.

Not a question of ability, but purely of fitness. I had had an attack of jaundice only a few weeks earlier and this may have reduced my resistance to those long, active hours in the sun.

Bowlers must get to bed early, but an out-of form batsman can often find the relaxation he has lacked by an evening out with the boys. But don't ask the skipper first, because you might still make a duck the following day!

*Fielding* is not a bore, but it is up to the individual to maintain his own interest during long hours in the field. At Barbados in 1960 we fielded for more than two days, eleven or twelve hours without ever getting a wicket! Looking at the clock does you no good on those occasions. In fact, they say in county cricket that once you start clock-watching you may as well give up the game.

I had been a more enthusiastic than efficient fielder for my four years in county cricket when we sailed to the West Indies. Imagine my surprise and great satisfaction and delight when Peter May asked me to think in terms of fielding cover-point for the whole tour. I was determined to make a success of the job and practised fielding and throwing as much as batting and bowling.

Once on the field I resolved to field every ball as fast and efficiently as possible, regardless of the state of the game and paying no attention to the batsmen's call. It is so easy to imagine that the batsmen will not take a run, and then find yourself a yard too slow with a chance of a run out as they scamper across.

I stick to the Rugby maxim of playing the ball and not the man. Countless runs can be saved and the occasional run out is worth all the vain ball-chasing.

Brian Statham and I managed to run out Sobers in the last innings of the third Test at Sabina Park on the 1959–60 tour, when we never looked like getting him out any other way, and he would surely have won the match had he stayed at the crease for another few overs. I repeat that fielding is not a bore to the good fielder.

*Googlies* have always been a rather fascinating and mysterious part of the art of leg spin bowling. They are akin to the art of the conjuror whose sleight-of-hand can mislead the keenest eye. Of course the bowler cannot distract the batsman's attention from the hand with the ball in it as would a conjuror, but he can definitely mislead the batsman, bowling an apparent leg break which turns from the off.

The best bowlers of the googly have had more than one type. Bruce Dooland would bowl a googly that the batsman would spot easily enough, and think himself that much more secure for knowing which way the ball would turn. But a few balls later, Bruce would produce just as efficient a googly, but much more cleverly disguised, which would be twice as effective because the batsman had become less cautious as a result of picking out the first one so easily.

Some cricketing terminology that even confuses the players at times concerns left-arm wrist-spin bowlers. Their ordinary delivery is called the Chinaman and the ball turns from the off to right-handed batsmen. The left-arm bowler can then bowl his own googly which turns from leg and is also known as the googly. It is sometimes called the 'bosie', particularly in Australia, nicknamed after a Mr Bosanquet who was one of the first effective googly bowlers.

*Hands* are the cricketer's most sensitive and vital contact with the whole game. We talk of a fielder with very good hands. He seems to pick up the most awkward bouncing ball, or the fastest travelling slip-catch perfectly cleanly with hardly ever a fumble. Tony Lock has the best hands I have ever seen. His

Hands 1. *Tony Lock almost nonchalantly scoops up the ball one-handed to dismiss Les Savill of Essex*

arms and hands are strong but they are not unusually large. He sometimes seems to strike at a passing ball almost as a snake strikes to kill, and the ball and hand will coincide perfectly to make a clean catch or field.

Big hands are a tremendous advantage to a catcher, but by no means all-important.

Alan Oakman catches a very high percentage of those catchable at first slip for Sussex. He has huge hands which between them can form almost a bucket-size cradle. He does not always catch the ball cleanly but has such a margin of error that he often juggles it safely into his open palms.

Quite the opposite is Philip Sharpe of Yorkshire who caught more than seventy catches in 1962, breaking the Yorkshire record for a season. He has small hands, and his reactions must be wonderfully accurate to catch successfully at first slip, especially to Fred Trueman's pace. I remember swinging at a ball on the leg side, getting a top edge which hit the 'keeper on the shoulder, and then flew out on the off side. Philip Sharpe could not have seen the ball till it appeared off the 'keeper's shoulder, but he held it safely and easily as though in a morning catching practice.

*Injuries* are frequent and unavoidable in cricket, so don't get the idea that it is a quiet game where nobody gets hurt.

Following the death of a boxer in the United States, surveys showed a high percentage of deaths on the cricket field, but I feel this is simply explained by the fact that club cricket is played, and often played best, by fairly old men.

Some players seem injury prone. Either they are awkward movers, brittle boned or just plain unlucky. Worcester were most unlucky to lose their two England bowlers, Flavell and Coldwell, at the vital moment when they were

Hands 2. *Stuart Surridge's massive hands dismiss Les Hamer of Derbyshire*

establishing a firm hold on the 1962 County Championship. Both were injured while fielding and probably through being tired after plenty of bowling that day.

Bowlers certainly get most muscular injuries, but fingers are more regularly broken taking catches and while batting.

No doubt fitness can avoid many injuries, but how do you account for Peter West's broken Achilles tendon?

He assures me he walked forward to pick up a stationary ball and heard the tendon snap like a banjo string.

This cricket must be more dangerous than I thought!

*Journalists*. My two favourite writers on any subject in the newspapers are both sporting writers, Jack Fingleton on cricket and John Lawrence on horse-racing. They both get the space and opportunity to write excellent English, and combine their literary talent with an intimate and well-informed knowledge of the game. No offence is meant to the many other writers who have similar opportunities to give full accounts of a day's cricket, or full coverage on team prospects, selection and so on, all of which are part of a cricket writer's business. It is worth getting one fact quite clear, that some writers for the daily newspapers are paid to give an account of the cricket as they saw it played from whatever point of vantage they may have gained.

Other writers are paid to go to a cricket match where there may be a large crowd and considerable excitement, and get a good story for their editor.

If the story is to be seen on the field of play so much the better. If it happens to be among the crowd or in the players' dressing-room it is still the story and not a cricketing account that must be told. So don't pick up the lighter English newspapers and expect to get a detailed account of the previous day's play. You will read a good story no doubt, but sometimes not very closely related to the game itself.

*Killer instinct* is normally spoken of when referring to a boxer who ruthlessly destroys his opponent. He knows well enough that it is either he or the other fellow who wins, and he cannot allow the other chap to come back once he has got him down. This killer instinct has been connected with my name on occasions, and though murder is far from my thoughts, I do feel I must play the game hard, particularly when I get into a winning position.

Cricket is such a whimsical game that a second's relaxation can mean a complete *volte face*, and the unpleasant experience of being the hunted rather than the hunter.

The batsman can show this sort of resolution by going on to make 200 rather than just a few more than 100.

The bowler can play it hard by exploiting a batsman's weakness, both technical and mental, playing perhaps on the memory of a previous dismissal at his hands. A batsman seldom gets out the same way twice to the same bowler, but he is often so concerned with avoiding that particular fate that he makes an even more simple error.

The captain owes it to his other ten players to play the game as hard as is reasonable within the rules, and within sanctions implied by the old phrase, 'It's not cricket'.

*Limbering up* is very important for bowlers and fielders before they get out on the field. Bowlers in England get worked very hard and muscles are bound to stiffen from day to day. The older you get the more important a few minutes' general exercise becomes before you have to make a fast uncontrolled move to field a ball and perhaps risk pulling a muscle.

If it is difficult to get out on the field just before the match, I have found that simple stretching exercises are just as effective. Leg injuries are usually in the groin or back of the thigh, and these muscles are very easy to stretch and it only takes a minute. Some bowlers like to get on the masseur's table for fifteen minutes before the game begins. If they have a troublesome injury, no doubt this is the best treatment for them, but for just plain stiff, tired muscles, a couple of minutes' stretching will do everything that a masseur can do.

I don't want to do any masseur out of a job—they certainly have a rightful and helpful part to play in keeping a side fit and out on the field, but I do believe that their job starts with genuine injuries, when the very best medical advice should be available, together with the best of masseurs to do any massage, manipulation or lamp work.

*Managers* of cricket sides are not quite so common as in other games. The M.C.C. appoint a manager to travel with teams sent abroad, for no captain could possibly undertake the complete organization of his side's travel, accommodation and general welfare, in addition to his considerable responsibilities on the field.

I do not believe that a manager need have any great knowledge of the game. He should be an able administrator who can mix socially at all levels, and who will personally gain the respect of those with whom he has to deal. The manager should have the final word on every matter connected with the tour whether cricketing or otherwise, because he has been chosen as a man whose judgment is above reproach and by whose decisions the whole tour must either stand or fall.

The manager gains most respect from the players if he has a flair for organization which materially eases the strains of a tour.

There are bound to be hitches making arrangements for twenty people of

New Ball. *A very hostile David Larter bowls to Mushtaq*

vastly differing tastes and temperaments, but if each individual can believe that the manager has their personal welfare at heart, and can see concrete evidence to that effect, then he will work his hardest to support the manager when the passage is a big rough.

'*New ball*' shouts the umpire to the batsman and then shows it with proper ceremony held high to the scorer far away in the box. This is the signal for the fast bowlers to come back into action. They may be trying to break a partnership well established against the spinners, or perhaps to bowl out the tail-end batsmen. The new ball may be taken at varying times depending on the duration of the game, and in what country it is being played.

The effect of a new ball is often quite electrifying. The old ball, worn rough by perhaps eighty or ninety overs, may bounce slowly and low off the wicket. It has become soft and gives the bowlers little encouragement. Then they feel the new hard ball, shiny with the fresh stitched seam and they feel new hope and confidence. For those first few overs the ball will skip quickly and bounce relatively high off the most docile wicket.

The batsman must be ready for the sudden change and try to weather these first few overs. He may even have made sure of not getting out in the previous overs before the new ball became due, in order to see off the shine himself and not let the fast bowlers have a go at a new batsman. More in cricket than meets the eye perhaps?

*Opportunity* never knocks twice, and a cricketer should remember those few words like his own name. The road to an England cap is dependent upon selection and not on your own efforts alone. Thousands of runs and wickets are no sure way to a place in the England side. That decision is purely up to those selectors who sit round on a Sunday morning to pick a side for the coming Test Match. From among hundreds of cricketers the selectors may find reason to choose you to play for England. Remember that many players have played only once for England—some of them have seized their one opportunity and performed with great success only to find their name omitted from a similar side only a couple of weeks later.

This must be a bitter pill to swallow, but much worse would be the thought that you had not given everything you knew when that opportunity came your way.

To keep a place in the England side is often a chancy business, but you can help to keep luck on your side by working for the team both on and off the field. The tour to the West Indies in 1960 was remarkable for the good spirits and hard work of each individual—many of those sent on that tour have retained their place for England in subsequent seasons and they have certainly earned that honour.

*Padding and protection* are vital to the cricketer. Wicket-keepers get broken hands despite wearing layers of gloves and tape round their finger joints. Batsmen's legs and thighs get bruised and painful despite heavy pads on both places. Batsmen also wear abdominal protection which saves them from serious injury, although often not from considerable pain when struck in that area. It is well worth-while getting the best protection that money can buy. Those very light spiked-rubber strips on cotton gloves have gone out of fashion, although older players will swear they never had a finger injury while wearing them. They were replaced by sausage-type horse-hair protection, and now lightweight plastic foam is being given a trial.

Old photographs certainly show a rather frightening lack of padding which makes me wonder whether the players were tougher or the bowlers slower or

Padding and Protection. *Neil Harvey equipped with 'sausage-type' gloves, leg guards and a thigh pad—watched by John Murray, equally well protected*

the balls not so hard.

One gentleman used to have his pads pumped up with a bicycle pump by his personal servants. Perhaps that was why they changed the leg-bye rule. The batsman must play a shot at the ball to be allowed a run off his pads. The gentleman with the blown-up pads may well have registered a six with a well directed boot at a ball going down the leg side.

*Quick bowling* is surely one of the best sights in cricket—the bowler going flat out and every ball a possible wicket. I remember what a thrill it was watching England play South Africa at Lord's more than ten years ago.

Bill Edrich took his long run bowling from the pavilion end and knocked one of Dudley Nourse's stumps flying out of the ground with the first ball of the day. That was thrilling enough, but imagine the excitement when Denis Compton, fielding on the boundary, walked over to us small boys and said: 'That was a surprise for all of us.'

I remember asking him for his autograph, but, just as I have to do myself, he had to refuse a signature while actually on the field. It's not because I don't want to sign, but because giving one signature is the signal for all the other autograph hunters to run across and try to get one, too. There just isn't time to do so many, even in the interval between batsman going out and coming in, and it is better not to start the ball rolling.

Incidentally don't judge a fast bowler's speed until you have watched him from the side, and remember that the type of wicket makes a big difference. Even I can look quite quick on a grassy firm wicket where the ball skips off fast and lively. But Wesley Hall can look fast on a slow soft wicket where I would not even reach the wicket-keeper standing back. So watch a fast bowler more than once before making up your mind how fast he bowls.

*Running* between the wickets is not given nearly enough attention even by the best batsmen. Only half the runs scored in cricket are by boundaries. You have to run up and down that twenty-yard strip for all the others. I have never seen a batsman practising a quick turn at the ends, yet a good turn can mean all the difference between one and two runs.

We talk about a batsman being a good judge of a run, and it is a pleasure to bat with Colin Cowdrey. Colin will play a ball softly and be off up the wicket, having called you as he plays the ball. Very often we have crossed and are in at the opposite ends before the fielder has even picked up the ball, let alone thrown it in.

The non-striking batsman should watch the striker's face and never watch where the ball has gone if it is forward of the striker's wicket.

As a general rule he should always run when the striker calls him, but he

Running. *Cape Town, 1957. The classic example of bad running. Tayfield and Van Ryneveld caught at the same end. Godfrey Evans turned, rolled the ball along the ground and scored a direct hit to run out Tayfield*

still has the right to send him back, and a loud 'No' immediately following the striker's 'Yes' will usually give the striker time to get back to his own end.

Lastly, never give up even if you are both stranded in the middle of the wicket. The fielder can still make a mistake, and in fact often does in the excitement.

*Scorers* are vital to the game and it is important that a proper record is kept of every match played. On Test Match grounds the scorers seem rather remote, but they have a job in which they cannot afford to make a mistake. Very often they also have to control a huge scoreboard, with various helpers, keeping bowlers' analyses up to date, flashing lights to signify who has fielded the ball, besides interpreting every signal from the umpire.

In Sussex we are very lucky to have George Washer whose accuracy and statistical knowledge of Sussex cricket is quite phenomenal.

I believe the Australian Test Match scorers actually make a record of where every batsman scores his runs off each particular bowler, a system begun by

Bill Ferguson. This could be a tremendous help both to the home batsmen and even more so to the captain and bowlers in trying to curb the opposing side's best shots. The best players can obviously score runs all round the wicket, but they still have their favourite shots and to curb these is most important to the fielding side.

*Touring* abroad with the M.C.C. or on one of the shorter trips organized by Jim Swanton or Ron Roberts must be the goal of every cricketer. First-class cricket in England is itself hard work, with its six-day week and big matches over the main holidays, so tours come quite easily to the England cricketer. There are days set aside for travel and practice which may allow some free time for sight-seeing, golfing or swimming. You feel pretty good when you get away to a place like Palm Beach outside Sydney, the guest of some kind person interested in cricket, and then think that you are missing an English winter— all at someone else's expense!

I could fill a book with the names of people who have been generous to me

Touring. *One of the delights of touring. Fred Trueman on a Trinidad beach*

**Umpires.** *Sid Buller, one of our **top** umpires*

and others of the teams I have travelled with, but perhaps they will accept this general thank-you from me for all their hospitality.

*Umpires* get nothing but kicks. A soccer or rugby referee can come off the field knowing that he has handled the game well and that this fact will almost certainly be mentioned in press reports on the following day. I have never seen it in print that two umpires handled a cricket match particularly well, and I don't suppose I ever will. But times without number both players and reporters find reason to complain of, or to query, umpires' decisions.

It is hard for a bowler to accept a 'not out' decision when he feels sure that he had the fellow lbw, or for a batsman to walk out unconcerned when given out leg before when he knew he hit the ball first. The fact to remember is that the best umpire in the world will occasionally make a mistake and therefore the players must always behave civilly towards every umpire, whatever their opinion of his judgment.

One further thought about umpiring may be worth suggesting to those just starting the job: A 'not out' decision gives all concerned another chance, whereas once the umpire raises his index finger to send a batsman on his way to the pavilion, his decision is final and allows no second chance. He should be mighty certain of the facts before giving that irrevocable decision.

*Volunteers* are hard to come by for the less pleasant jobs in cricket. One of the less pleasant, surely, is the job of nightwatchman—the lower order batsman in whom the captain has most faith as a defensive batsman. He has to go in only a few minutes before the end of play with the one intention of staying there until the umpires call an end to the day's activities. (It was Alec Skelding who would say after the winning stroke on the second day of a county match, 'And that, gentlemen, completes three days' entertainment—in two.')

Down in Sussex I have been lucky to have one or two ambitious batsmen who reckon they should be higher up the order. Often they ask me earlier in the day if they can do nightwatchman should the occasion arise and I cannot refuse any volunteer for what I would consider a rotten job. Ronnie Bell has been a stalwart for Sussex in this position, apart from all the other positions he has batted for us in previous years. Ian Thomson is also a contender for the job. He came to Sussex as a batsman originally and has played a host of wonderful innings for us, although we are still waiting for his maiden century.

There have been some amusing nightwatchmen incidents, not the least of which was Jim McConnon's effort playing for Glamorgan against Cambridge. As Jim is left-handed the field had to change round a good deal before Gami Goonesena could bowl the next ball.

Short third man to the right-hander was moved down to long leg, but it was the end of a long day, so he was taking his own time going down to the boundary. Gami bowled his ordinary spinner turning in to Jim McConnon, who obviously thought attack would be the best way of surviving. He swung to leg and skied it round the corner. A shout to the back of the retreating long leg turned him round in time to take a nice catch. Nightwatchman caught halfway to the boundary off his first ball would cause comment in any dressing-room, and I'll bet there were a few well-chosen words flying round between those talkative Welshmen.

*Wives* of cricketers have helped their husbands at every level of the game. At village matches they appear to make the tea and prepare the sandwiches for their perspiring husbands. In club games they may prefer to grace the boundaries as a semi-attentive audience, but nevertheless a decorative addition to the day's entertainment.

Wives of first-class cricketers are in the news mostly under the well-worn heading of 'wives-on-tour'. For some time now there has been no objection to a player's wife spending part of a tour with her husband. My wife Susan came to the West Indies for three weeks, but this was completely at our own expense, so it is not the sort of thing you can arrange every day of the week. Wives are not very welcome at the outset of a tour when players are settling down and getting to know each other. Obviously if only one player had his wife with him

Wives. *Ted Dexter takes a turn at the barrel organ as he arrives at a charity show in London with his wife Susan. Watching is the Pearly Queen of Hampstead*

on the boat going abroad he would be enjoying a holiday with her, rather than mixing with his new team mates.

Rather than being envious, I have noticed players enjoying the arrival of a new face from England. A lady brings a little gentleness, and a breath of the outside world, things which can become rather forgotten among twenty men living and talking cricket over a period of months.

*X-rays* should be taken of any finger injury before trying to use any other treatment. So many people have been proved wrong after feeling a finger injury and called it 'just a bruise'. Anguished tales are told of fingers being pushed and pulled to ascertain whether they are broken, before X-rays have been allowed to play their simple part in the diagnosis.

X-ray photographs have exposed some frightening sights of wicket-keepers' hands, knocked about by years of catching. I believe the practice of taping all the top joints of the fingers with non-elastic tape is modern in origin and 'keepers may now perhaps keep their hands in better shape. Old photographs also show very small gloves with no apparent room for finger guards or a reasonable thickness of padding. They look more like ordinary driving gauntlets than gloves specially designed for the job.

A faint crack in a top finger joint should not cause too much concern. The only danger in continuing to play would be the greater damage done by another blow on the same finger.

I think this risk is worth taking and if the finger is not more tender than a bad bruise would be, then you should report fit for play.

*Young cricketers* are the luckiest of the lot. Why? Because they still have all the fun to come.

Young batsmen have a problem in that they cannot yet have the strength to play all the shots, and yet hitting the ball hard to the boundary is a very tempting goal to aim at. They should not sacrifice control of the bat and proper shot-making, just for the satisfaction of hitting the occasional four to square leg. The bowlers have a real problem that can be insoluble. Many young slow bowlers reach a very high standard at the age of 14 and 15. Alan Duff was as good a leg spinner at 14 years of age as you would wish to see. He was at Radley College with me and came to school with authenticated tales of bowling out Worcester Club and ground sides. His father had taught him all he knew and encouraged him all the time.

He was not very tall at that age, and threw the ball up in the air to get it up to a good length the other end. Then he started to grow taller and stronger. His fingers grew longer, needing a change of grip on the ball. As he grew taller those good length balls, bowled by him at the same angle, became full tosses. Within a year his skill had left him completely.

He continued to play high-class cricket at Oxford as a fine batsman and a fair leg spinner. The answer would be to grade the size of ball and length of wicket throughout boys' schooling. If a boy were too big and bowled too fast for the shorter pitch he would be moved up a grade.

Only in this way would genuine talent of the prodigy-type be able to flourish in the best way.

Alan Duff would have spun his leg breaks with a small ball and on an eighteen-yard wicket. As he grew, a bigger ball and longer wicket would have kept pace with his physical development, and England might well have had a high-class leg spinner for the first time in many years.

*Z*——. Who ever heard of anything to do with cricket beginning with Z? I-Zingari, the famous club? But that begins with I. Howzat—but that begins with H. No Zany or Zoo inhabitant has played the game lately. Yes, you've guessed it, I've lost my Zest for this chapter.

*Chapter 5*

# DEAD OR ALIVE

CRICKET is no more dying than I am. Club cricket in England is flourishing with more registered clubs than ever before. New pavilions are being opened and new grounds acquired, financed by a wide variety of individuals and organizations. Some say that few youngsters are joining their local clubs—perhaps they are enjoying their extra earned pounds in other ways—but they may well revert to cricket as they settle down within a village community.

Attendances at first-class cricket fixtures fell from nearly two and a half million in 1947 to only just over a million in 1960. But these figures show only those who paid at the gate. During these same years, membership of the various county clubs has shown almost as startling a rise. Money has been pouring into the game from other sources. It may seem an unsound way to finance cricket by football pools, but if people are willing to pay money that way, where is the harm?

Glamorgan has been able to create a fund which virtually assures the future of the club. At Old Trafford, the pavilion has been rebuilt, and new accommodation and facilities provided for members and public. This hardly seems possible within the framework of a dying game.

The Warwickshire County Club has been transformed into the most go-ahead organization during the last ten years. The ground has become one of the best appointed in the world, and construction work there is not finished yet. The fact that they went close to winning the Championship in 1962 was due reward for all their hard work.

At Hove, the pavilion has been rebuilt throughout for Sussex members, and

71

now the hotel at the entrance gates is newly constructed, offering a fine dining-room with a view of the cricket. None of these things was considered at a time when twice the number of people were passing through the gates to watch.

Nobody would deny that our society is changing fast, and if the game is supported by pools and television, rather than a paying public, it is surely only what that same public have wanted and created. And even if the pools system were to collapse, the interest in high-class cricket is still great enough to support the game.

Yearly membership subscription to the county clubs is still amazingly low and bears no relation to the amenities and entertainment provided. Some people have been proud to tell me that they are members of all the home county cricket clubs. If they can afford to do that, they are certainly being asked for too little by their own county club.

If they were asked for a sensible contribution toward the running of the club I foresee various satisfactory outcomes. Everyone wants value for money, so the club would be well supported on all occasions when matches were played at home. Friendships would grow apace, doing almost as much good for the club as the inevitable and probably spectacular rise in bar profits. Members would be able to demand proper facilities, and they would get a hearing because their money would be the life-blood of the club. Committees would have to work hard and satisfy the members, because there would always be members willing to have a go at administering their own and other people's money.

There is one thing that members would also be rightly able to demand, and that would be the sort of cricket they want to watch.

A little earlier I said that the low subscriptions bear little relationship to the amenities and entertainment provided. I regret that sometimes the entertainment is not worth more than the money paid, but this is not the fault of the players. If the member paid more, there would be more money to pay the players, and there would be more competition for the good salaries earned. At the moment cricketers' salaries are very modest, far too little to attract the talented young man away from a quite ordinary business position with good prospects.

I was lucky enough to be on the Committee of the famous Cambridge University club 'The Hawks'. The subscriptions had not been changed in thirty years, while the pound was buying only a quarter of what it used to. The club was best frequented at lunch time, only because it offered a cheap and good lunch. There was hardly any club activity, and it was like a morgue in the evening. The simple business of maintaining the club building was becoming a serious headache to the treasurer.

It was decided to raise the subscriptions, and though they were raised to only a fraction of the relative level paid years before, interest in the club improved immediately. Members wanted to get their money's worth and frequented the place. New friends were made, meetings, appointments and dinners took place in the club. A snooker competition was enthusiastically played and a boat arranged to watch the bumping races on the river.

Perhaps those extra few pounds pinched the odd pocket, but the dividends for all concerned were colossal.

Cricket clubs could be just as lively as the Hawks club became for those few years, and, I trust, ever since.

The pools system is keeping the cricket club subscriptions down at a completely false level. It has done the game good, and kept it going over a difficult period, but if the pools system were now to collapse either of its own accord, or by pressure of members to pay for and run their own club, it would surely be for the better.

The clubs that are most hard hit by the present system are those that have no pool, or an ineffective one. They cannot raise their subscriptions to a proper level because there would be an outcry from those whose friends pay only half the amount in the neighbouring county.

The interest is there, and the money is in every man's hands as it has never been before. If the two were put together, then cricket could forget financial worry.

Imagine the situation if the top class cricketer could command a salary of £3,000 from his club. Every young cricketer in the country would be competing for such a coveted position. That sum may sound a great deal, but it hardly compares with the earnings of a high-class American baseball player, or continental soccer player. The player would have to produce the goods and entertain the members, or someone would soon take his place.

At present a lad who joins a county staff and makes his way into the first team may not be more than an average player, yet he can keep his place in the side through lack of competition.

More money, more interest and better cricket would all be complementary, and I believe that more money from members is the right end to start.

So much for our national cricketing programmes, but cricket is even more alive on the international level and in other cricketing countries.

The five-day crowd which attended Old Trafford to watch England play Australia in 1961 was a record one. They saw a fascinating match where the game fluctuated violently until the last ball was bowled.

Davidson made runs quickly. David Allen took quick wickets and he was hit for sixes. I hit quick runs. Benaud took quick wickets, and was hit for six, and people say that Test cricket is not what it used to be!

More than two million spectators witnessed the M.C.C. play in India, Pakistan and Ceylon over a period of only four months. The M.C.C. made a very handsome profit to be distributed to the counties, and the host countries profited greatly, too.

*Allen took quick wickets . . . Mackay caught Close 18*

*Benaud was hit for 6 . . . a full-blooded drive by Close*

Advance bookings for the series in Australia over the winter 1962–3 are, at the moment of writing, far in advance of England's last tour to that part of the world. The game is attracting more attention from every type of person than ever before.

This growing interest has been reflected by the daily newspapers who have considered it necessary to give the game increasing coverage. This has had one most unfortunate effect. Many more correspondents accompanied the M.C.C. to Australia in 1958 than had ever done before. All these writers were forced into competition with each other, not only in literary talent, but in story-finding.

Demands became more and more sharp from editors in England. 'Why have you failed to tell the "absent player" story as reported in a rival newspaper?' or similar demands. Writers cannot vie with one another to write the more glowing report, as they soon become sickly and unreadable. They can, and must, vie with each other to tell the most eye-catching tale.

'Cricket is dying' makes a better headline than 'Cricket is thriving', and that is the way it has to be written regardless of the facts. Nevertheless the immense coverage and publicity given the game has had a lot to do with the more general public interest.

Perhaps the cutting down of the number of newspapers in Fleet Street will lessen the direct competition between papers and lead to a less sensational type of account.

In my short time as a county and England captain, I have found the 'Gentlemen of the Press' very reasonable to deal with as long as I do not expect too much.

It may be worth recording the sort of thing that one has to put up with in terms of misreporting. Following the selection of the side to Australia in 1962, I was asked to give the Press a few answers to straightforward questions.

'Will you make special arrangements for practice for your team?'

'Yes,' I replied. 'We have four fast bowlers to keep fit, and those not playing must do some work in the nets. We will ask for good nets to be available, particularly at Melbourne.'

I was thinking of the fact that Melbourne has no nets on the ground, and players have to go by car to a neighbouring school who make their nets available. It would take that much extra organization to get them to practice.

A few days later I was called to the telephone. 'Have you heard that your critical remarks of Melbourne's practice facilities have been relayed to Ian Johnson, who runs the Melbourne Ground? He was told of what you said, and was most upset at your remarks.'

I was distressed that my remark had been misconstrued in such a way, and asked that apologies should be sent to all concerned. I wrote immediately to Ian Johnson, telling him the true content, and intention of my remarks, assuring him that I remembered the excellent arrangements made for us in 1958.

Ian Johnson soon replied saying that he had heard my remarks, and agreed that it was a pity no practice nets were available on the ground, but that he would make arrangements for practice as before.

See what I mean? Don't expect anyone to be too accurate, and don't get too worried if a bad report comes through.

Only when a cricketer demands absolute fairness and accuracy from the

Press, from his point of view, or when a writer tries to maintain that he believes every word he writes to be the only possible accurate and fair account of the facts, do feelings get hurt and tempers frayed.

The public, even one's own personal friends, are the most difficult to get educated in this way. They will watch a match and sometimes complain bitterly the next day that their newspaper is inaccurate and unfair to certain players, but when those same friends have not watched a game, and read some criticism of players, they are very likely to believe every word.

The power of the written word is not only strong, it is positively hypnotic. Once written, however unlikely the content of the words, they take on an aura of truth which it is very difficult to disregard.

In the other cricketing countries of the world the game continues to flourish. In the West Indies it is a delight to experience the interest in cricket of almost every individual of the population.

We arrived one sunny morning in Barbados, the first small piece of land

*Ian Johnson, who now runs the Melbourne Cricket Ground*

seen for about a week's sailing. Lined up on the quayside was a tremendous welcoming crowd, every member competing with his neighbour in the quite difficult task of recognizing players who were known previously only by their photographs.

I remember driving away through a cheering throng of well-wishers immediately behind another car in which Peter May was sitting. As we cleared the crowd a lone Barbadian stood on the pavement. He recognized the occupant of the leading car, reverently removed his hat, and said quite loudly, but to no one in particular, 'It's Peter May!'

The common ground in the cities is used for as many cricket matches as can fit in the space, and many is the time that the cars slow down as makeshift wickets are removed from the middle of the road, and cricket temporarily—and grudgingly—suspended.

The West Indian has an amazing natural ability for the game, and he seems to adopt the tricks of the trade as though he had known them from birth. The first time Seymour Nurse batted against the M.C.C. he made over two hundred.

*Seymour Nurse drives Illingworth through the covers, watched by Cowdrey and wicket-keeper Swetman*

*Groundsmen clearing up after the demonstration at Port of Spain*

He played sensibly and surely, technically well and with great assurance, from the first ball he received to the last. He played the sort of cricket that it would take most people years to learn how to play, even if they had the ability.

The crowds were spectacular in their appreciation of the game. Four wide balls left alone by the batsman would incite yells of 'Bowl at the wicket', and not the dreary slow handclap that might come from the Tavern on a Saturday afternoon. And all the spectators sitting near the front have done so in order to be able to talk to the boundary fielder.

Who is the fastest bowler in the world? Who's the best batsman in the world? What about O'Neill? What about Adcock? The questions come thick and fast from behind the concentration-camp type wire netting which contains the cheaper ring spectators.

I remember being grateful for those stout wire nettings at Port of Spain when the bottle-throwing incident stopped play for the day. It was not the sort of thing that could ever have happened at a dying game.

Only a large crowd whose passions were roused and closely involved could possibly have made such a violent demonstration. It would be wrong to imagine that the bottle-throwing proved a wholly partisan attitude, even though the outburst came when things were going very hard for the West Indians.

The reception that English players received when they made runs, fielded or bowled particularly well was always most generous. Though it probably sounded sweeter in my ears, I know that the applause for my hundred at Barbados was every bit as loud and sincere as that which acclaimed the greater feats of batsmanship by Sobers and Worrell later in that match.

In India and Pakistan the new nationalism drives the crowds in their thousands to watch their chosen gladiators do battle with the invaders from abroad. And the people are always willing to make their own amusement when the cricket is not up to standard.

But it is not always lack of interest in the cricket that touches off some of the more diverting crowd incidents over there.

The ladies are normally segregated into a stand of their own, and of course we always tried to send the best looking among us to field nearest them on the boundary. Being a captain, I could never get that far afield, and I always wonder what some of those young ladies said to make the boys blush so often!

The ladies' stand was usually gaily decorated with canopies of gorgeous hues, and the variety of coloured saris worn by the watchers tended to attract the eye to that part of the ground.

The eye was not the only thing these ladies attracted, because, about once a day, the male audience standing either side of the ladies' enclosure would

*Dexter, surrounded by police and spectators during the demonstration in the second Test at Port of Spain. In the background are a few of the bottles thrown by the crowd*

rebel against the composure of the weaker sex and take steps to discomfort them. Dust bombs were their favourite weapons, the necessary ingredient being by no means hard to find in that thirsty country. Water bombs were more scarce, but not unknown. The victims would scatter like chaff before the wind.

A minor diversion such as this would probably spark off something more entertaining to the original contestants, and pitched battle might soon be waged between two sections of the crowd. They would split apart, leaving a waste battle ground that nobody dared to tread on for fear of a well-directed stoning.

Come the evening, huge bonfires burned on the concrete terraces, perhaps only to replace the light purposely reflected into the batsmen's faces by mirrors

81

while the sun had been higher in the sky.

It was at Ahmedabad that the loudest crackers were tossed under the boundary fielders' feet. At Kanpur, known in the times of British Sovereignty as Cawnpore, Polly Umrigar was felled by a well-directed and catapulted unripe lemon. Fielders wisely remained twenty yards within the boundary, hoping that the crowd would throw back the ball following a boundary, and hoping that catapults had been put away for the day. More likely, the crowd would laugh at such timidity, and refuse to return the ball except when urged by a policeman's bayonet from behind.

At Madras, a section of the crowd played cymbals, drums and trumpets without the slightest break, as loud as they knew how, for every playing minute of the five-day Test Match. It was at Madras that the coach taking us from the ground was lucky to get through, whilst a heavy blow on the side of the head by a thrown orange taught me once and for all that windows were for closing.

These incidents could hardly have happened to a dying game. The disappointment of those crowds that they were denied a sight of Statham, Trueman, Flavell, May, Cowdrey and Graveney was touching in its sincerity. Perhaps they will not be denied when the M.C.C. next travel in that part of the world.

I have not had the good fortune to travel or play cricket anywhere on the continent of Africa, but reports from English cricketers come thick and fast about the fine grounds, good cricket and a host of new countries beginning to play the game keenly and well.

Africa may be the continent of the future, a new world power and political bloc, and it is well to realize the immense cricket potential that lies untouched there, apart from hidden mineral and agricultural resources.

I have written my way across the world toward Australia. Cricket is played in Ceylon and Malaya at a well-organized and competitive, though not international, level. It is played in Scotland and Ireland, Holland, Denmark, Hong Kong, Canada, South America, British Honduras, California, and a thousand other places where cricketers can find the space and time to have a game.

Why should any of these countries not become a great power at cricket? If they do I shall be the first to applaud them. My world tour of cricket as a lively, healthy game has now reached its natural climax in Australia.

I write as the 1962–3 M.C.C. Touring Team are on the way to that great cricketing country. The Aussies deserve a book to themselves, and must now at least have their own chapter.

## Chapter 6

# THE AUSSIES

THE morning of a Test Match against Australia is just that much more tense than any other day for English cricketers.

In 1961, the photographer, Henri Cartier Bresson, asked to spend a few days with me to take photographs of my normal working day in the cricket season. He came to Sussex on the train, took photographs in the nets, and in the dressing-room—anything to produce a picture story. I found him an interesting and charming man to whom conversation came easily and we managed to entertain each other adequately for the first day or two.

On the third day I was due to drive to Birmingham for the first Test Match against the Australians. I do not believe my French friend knew what he was getting involved in when he said he would accompany me. Thoughts of the impending game came crowding into my mind as we drove up the M1. Conversation became strained, limited to yes-and-no answers. At one moment he asked whether I always drove so fast, and I was surprised to see the speedometer well up over the 80 mark. I drove him to the match on the following morning, and my conversation had dried up completely.

I do hope that Monsieur Bresson understood that it was those Aussies who restrained my talking, and that I was not suddenly bored by his company.

The Aussies have a reputation for playing their games hard, and it is an enviable reputation to have. The toughness of Australian cricket comes from their playing less cricket than we do in England. Because they play less, every match becomes that much more important to the individual. They do not feel as we do in England, 'If we fail today, we are going to have another knock tomorrow, and another a couple of days later.' Each game is more important to them, and they may show that little extra resolution, particularly against the M.C.C. tourists.

Nothing is nicer in England than making runs and taking wickets against the touring side, whoever they may be. Bernie Constable of Surrey must be the most consistent scorer against tourists in England, and you don't have to look at him twice to see how much pleasure he gets out of it. Nor are the Australians shy to show their pleasure in twisting the lion's tail on the cricket field.

In England one county plays nearly every other county twice in the season. We play six days a week. It is more like a travelling circus. There is more camaraderie in the game—though people play hard enough when the chips are down.

Abroad, the whole thing is that much more intense, because many of the opposing players have only one crack at you. They are flat out to do well, and perhaps gain the favour of their selection committee.

This intense individual concern with success or failure makes for some poor cricket. Not only the individual, but the whole team are often pleased that one man gets a hundred at the expense of the match—a contest which both sides should be trying to win.

In India and Pakistan there was only one game outside the Test series where the other side gave us a chance of winning, and so gave themselves a similar chance. Some say that this sort of cricket on the last day of a match is too contrived, and not genuine cricket, and yet afternoon club cricket matches have been played on that principle for as many years as the game has been played. Side A may win the toss, and put side B in to bat. Side B scores over two hundred for only four wickets down, but makes a declaration which should give both sides an equal chance of winning. Contrived? It is just acceptable Saturday afternoon cricket.

The Nawab of Pataudi captained a side against the M.C.C. at Hyderabad and made a good declaration, leaving us just over two hundred to make in about two hours. The M.C.C. won the game in the last few minutes after being five wickets down in the first hour. I honestly thought we would lose. The crowd were thrilled at the excitement of the last ten minutes' play, and yet hardly another match on the whole tour was played wholeheartedly to win by both sides.

Before going to Australia in 1962 I tried to get an advance word through to our opponents in the two-day games, hoping that the matches would be played to fighting finishes. The M.C.C. do not mind losing a game, and surely the thrill for an up-country XI at beating an M.C.C. side would far outweigh seeing the local champion making a hundred against us at the expense of the game itself.

Other than this question of less cricket, I do not think the cricket in Australia is tougher than in England. There are few enough games in England, even on a Sunday afternoon, where you can idle your way through without a bit of needle creeping in.

Benaud is certainly a daunting opponent because he has had such tremendous success. He has done wonders for the game of cricket. He has a great sense of the occasion. You could call it showmanship and I think you would be right, but it is just the right sort of showmanship, and the sort that cricket needs. If two captains of his type can co-operate in a cricket match, they can produce the lively cricket that crowds appreciate with never any question of cooking the books.

Some of our Test players have played under Richie on international tours, and they say he would literally sacrifice a game for the sake of a grandstand finish, and then have supreme confidence that his players would pull it out of the bag when the time came.

In England, I sometimes thought his confidence had put him in a hopeless position, and would lose him the game. I certainly thought he had lost at Manchester when I was batting. I was scoring quickly and he went on trying to get me out when most captains would have tried to shut the game up. He never set the field back, or asked any bowler to bowl defensively and stop the scoring. He used every bowler in turn to orthodox field placings, in fact played every trick he knew.

His last card turned up trumps when he went round the wicket himself, and had me caught by the incomparable Wally Grout. I am pleased to note that I am walking out without looking at the umpire, in a photograph which shows Wally with ball in hand, and the appeal ringing out loud and clear in true Aussie style.

Wally and I had an amusing chat on another occasion, when he was 'keeping to Richie's bowling at Leeds. Richie bowled a beauty, pitching leg, beating the bat, and missing the off stump. A terrific appeal from Wally and Richie together practically convinced me I had hit the ball, though I knew I had not. The umpire was not convinced either and gave me not out.

Wally came in for a drink that evening. 'You didn't really think I hit that did you, Wally?' I asked. 'No, no, Ted,' he replied. 'Just clearing my throat.'

No doubt he will 'clear his throat' many more times before he finishes his career in partnership with the twin menace of Davidson and Benaud. Richie has been lucky to have so many exceptionally talented players in his side—the

*Caught Grout bowled Benaud 76: Dexter 'walks' without waiting for the umpire's signal*

sort of players who can pull out something extra when it is really needed.

Two last wicket partnerships of about a hundred on the last trip to England in the two Test Matches won by Australia testify to this all-round ability of Richie's side.

Richie is that sort of cricketer himself, starting as a batsman, and finding a flair for leg spin bowling later on. Richie is no great spinner of the ball, but he bowls it high, has natural flight, bowls an excellent line, and gets plenty of bounce in Australia. He has a wide variety of balls, including the 'flipper'.

I think Bruce Dooland was the first successful 'flipper' bowler. It is bowled as you might spin a billiard ball down the table, the thumb starting under the wrist, and coming forward. It is an off break wrist action, with the hand dropped below the wrist instead of cocked above it. It can look just like a leg break and yet only has some 'under' off-spin if you see what I mean. The ball skids on quickly and may even come into the batsman from the off, which makes life a bit tricky if he imagines it will bounce and turn from leg!

Leg spinners of this type are almost impossible to find or bring into the game in England. Our wickets are never hard like a table top, and it is only on those wickets that the ball will hop on and bounce. A short ball in England bounces slowly and is soon on its way for four, but Richie gets wickets with short balls at Melbourne which can bounce head high! When he comes to England he is experienced enough to get his wickets despite the lack of local help.

It rains much more in England, and on such wickets the orthodox bowler is the best, so they are a must in any side. Our orthodox spinners may appear to be less aggressive than leg spin and googly bowlers. They may not beat the bat so often with an exceptional ball, but they can bowl accurately to a particular field, and make scoring comparatively difficult. They either get wickets for themselves or they get wickets for others by their economy.

The tempo may not be quite so lively as a leg spinner, who is either getting wickets or giving runs away. The leg spinner may be more spectacular, but I am not sure that this can be argued as the most effective way of getting people out. After all, there is quite a lot of time at your disposal in a five-day Test, and the result depends on how much it costs you to get batsmen out, not on how quickly you do it.

They have a similar saying in golf for the moderate golfer who is holing putts as against the good golfer who hits the green in one less, but finishes it in one more than his opponent—'It's not how, it's how many'.

English batsmen get precious little practice at wrist spin bowling, and this puts them psychologically at a disadvantage, but they have done none too

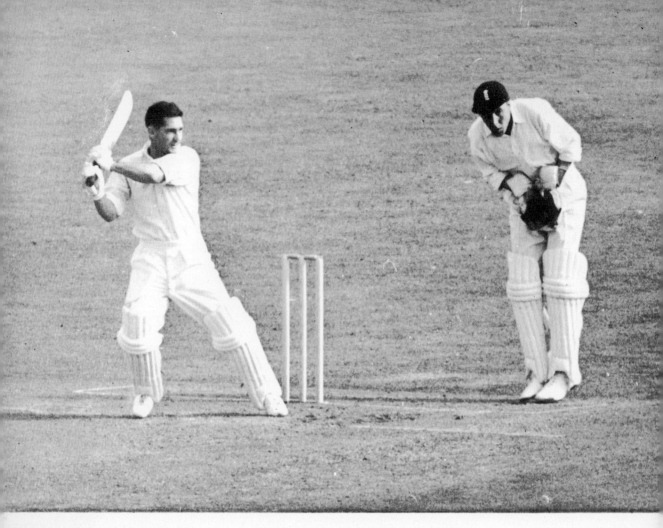

*Neil Harvey immaculately square cuts for 4*

badly against Benaud, Gupte, Borde and Sobers during the last five years.

One cannot talk about Australian cricket without thinking immediately of Bradman. Perhaps he will excuse me not titling him correctly as Sir Donald, but, as the best batsman of all time, the name I remember is Bradman. One can argue all day about Compton, Harvey, Hammond and Hutton, but Bradman averaged almost as many runs again as any of these. It is a similar statistic to the times of mile-runners, that prove conclusively that Elliot was a better miler than Wooderson.

Strange that nobody seems to remember Bradman for any particular shot. Compton would sweep the best spin bowlers to distraction, Hammond would hit them over extra cover, Peter May would bisect mid-wicket and mid-on with a powerful drive. They could all play the other shots as well, but it is for these individual skills that their names are specially remembered.

Bradman probably used to pull the short ball better than most, but then he hooked, cut and drove better than most, and so is only remembered for his phenomenal ability to make runs. Rather sad that the greatest of them all should be remembered in this somewhat unglamorous way. Maurice Tate was reported to have found him 'nothing out of the ordinary'. Nothing out of the ordinary except for the regular movement of the figures on the scoreboard from minute to minute, hour to hour, year to year.

Jardine and his fast bowling battery tried to curb him in the 'bodyline' tour. They succeeded, but Bradman still averaged many more than any of his

*Bradman—the greatest Australian batsman of all time. Leslie Ames is keeping wicket and Wally Hammond is at slip—quite a trio!*

compatriots. One hears no longer of Bradman's fielding. He may have been a good bowler for all I know, but I have never been told of a single ball he ever bowled, nor of a catch taken—just the mass of evidence written in the score-books to show that he was the best batsman the world has ever known.

Funny people the Australians. They have a deep-seated distrust of all those who come from England. The majority of their early written humour is directed at the English, and I ask Bill Wannan's permission to use a few extracts from his excellent treasury of Australian humour. There was violent discontent at the harsh systems of the penal colony run by the English Governors and Magistrates. England itself was a harsh and badly administered country at the time,

*Well held, Fred! Bill Lawry brilliantly caught by Trueman off Allen, but not before he had made 102 in the second innings at Manchester*

and the humour is directed at both the upper class in England and the English governing class in Australia. Bill Wannan writes:

'By the time of the 1880s, any sense of inferiority that may have been harboured originally by the local born Australians had long since given way to feelings of national pride.'

Arthur Patchett Martin wrote these lines at this time:

'No workhouse have we here,
No poor law coves so cruel,
No bullying overseer,
No paltry water gruel.
No Masters to oppress,
    A wretched starving devil,
But here, I rather guess,
    We're all upon a level.

'When great folks come, they find
    That labour's in the ascendant,
No cringing beggars mind
    But all are independent.
Their pride receives a blow
    Their greatness is a failure,
And to England back they go
    And run down poor Australia.'

He starts another narrative poem called 'My cousin from Pall Mall':

'There's nothing that exasperates a true Australian youth,
Whatever be his rank in life, be he cultured or uncouth,
As the manner of a London swell.'

And later of the same London swell:

'As he landed from the steamer at the somewhat dirty pier,
He took my hand, and lispingly remarked, "How very queer".'

The 'true Australian youth' murders his cousin from Pall Mall before many more lines of the poem are read.

These feelings are as strong today as they were in 1880, except that there is a great warmth and welcome to be enjoyed in Australia once they are satisfied that you are no 'Cousin from Pall Mall'.

Within weeks of my arrival in Australia there appeared in an evening paper

91

a longish article which started my nickname of Lord Edward.

Coming from a public school, and university, and living in London, I was immediately under suspicion as a 'London swell', or 'the man from Cambridge with an Oxford accent', an accent which was copied and spelled to the extent of writing 'beeah for bowlahs', and 'two leg please, Umpah'.

It was friendly enough comment, but it might as well have been written in 1880 by Arthur Patchett Martin.

You can be their greatest friend if you genuinely enjoy their company, find their beer good and their way of life attractive. But woe betide the Englishman who pretends to like the Australian and does not make the grade with him, because being patronized is not one of their favourite entertainments.

It is true that some people do return to England and run down Australia. 'I enjoyed my visit, but could not live there, could you?' They are entitled to live where they like, but they enjoyed their visit because they probably lived

*Bobby Simpson cuts*

off the fat of the land as guests of a most generous people.

Don't get in the back of a taxi in Australia, or you are likely to get taken halfway round the town and charged double. The drivers want you up the front for someone to talk to as much as anything else. Who else are they going to discuss their tax problems with, and it is not much fun having a beer on your own on a hot day. 'You from England? Well you better come and have a glass of our beer.' Taxi riding can become expensive, but seldom dull.

Hotel staff are usually cheerful enough workers, but again no respecters of persons. 'May I take your baggage, sir?' is strictly for the birds in the opinion of one hotel porter, who found it more homely to ask me whether my quite respectable suitcases were 'the muck you want taken up?'

The Australian Press seems to be a fine organization. Reporters are friendly and inquisitive, but are still employed for their knowledge of cricket as well as their journalistic capacity. It is said that they wage a clever campaign on the arrival of a team to break down the reputations of the touring players, and indeed do some of their Test sides' work for them in advance.

The answer to that must be first not to read the newspapers, and then to take enough wickets and make enough runs to leave nobody in any doubt that your reputation is deserved and even perhaps not quite so high as it should be.

I honestly said to one well-known journalist that I did not read any Press reports. He had started a constructive cricketing conversation by saying, 'You know the piece I wrote the other day—' I had to admit that I had not read his nor any other cricket report. He was shocked and tried to find good reasons why I should. The only rather lame reason he came up with, after some thought, was that I might get an objective viewpoint otherwise unavailable to me, and maybe pick up some good ideas. I agreed, but thought that there was a good chance of picking up a few bad ideas at the same time. To make it a worthwhile exercise, I should then have to read every report.

Anyway if I want an objective view, there are many people I could ask, including one or two of the pressmen whose opinions I would respect, given time for discussion. Not a bad rule for a captain might be to help the Press at every turn, and never read a word that is written thereafter.

What of the Australian crowds? 'Are they partisan?' Of course they are. 'Do they like seeing Australia licking England?' They love it. 'Are they rude to individuals?' You try and be ruder. 'Are they the best crowds in the world?' Very likely. They probably know their cricket as well as any, including the amazingly knowledgeable West Indians, but give them the right sort of cricket and they welcome you as one of their own.

A passion for horse racing makes up a large part of their conversation. Even

*Benaud bowled Dexter 2. A sweet moment during the fourth Test at Old Trafford, 1961*

a small transistor radio will pick up a race-by-race radio commentary from the various tracks, of which Randwick and Flemington must be the best known. On Saturday afternoons there is a special racing commentary from three tracks. The races are timed at ten minute intervals, 2, 2.10, 2.20 and so on, right through the afternoon. Heaven help the bank balance of anyone who feels he must bet on every race.

In Tasmania they even put down a dog track round the edge of the cricket field as soon as play has ended for the day. The previous touring side had been given excellent information by the groundsman, who was a real dog expert. Ten dogs raced at the same time on the big round track, so the information had to be pretty good.

We duly asked the groundsman for a few ideas when we got there, but he was loath to hazard an opinion. We finally nailed him down to one or two selections which ran nowhere. It was only the next day that we found out that it was not the same groundsman at all!

Almost the best memory of touring Australia is of the swimming, particularly on the beaches outside Sydney. Long shallow shelving beaches fully open to the Pacific where long swells move in with anything up to a hundred yards between crests. The Australians have developed the art of riding these rollers to perfection. They scorn the small surf board and use something more like a flat heavy canoe. So expert do they become that they stand on these as they race in toward the shore supported by the downward slope of the roller, which builds up to sixteen or twenty feet high, and surf riders experience terrific thrills as they race toward the beach.

I have since tried to find similar conditions in the West Indies, India, Pakistan, Colombo and Aden without much success. There may well be good spots on our own shores at home, but those other parts of the world spoil one for cold-water bathing.

I nearly drowned myself in Colombo, having found some goodish surf. Friends who were also learning had had enough and gone on the beach, while I foolishly had to have a few more tries.

I soon felt tired, and started to swim in, but seemed to be making little progress, except when the waves helped me. Fortunately I had the sense to keep my strength for the waves and get the utmost from their help, or I might not be here to tell the tale. I made the beach, and walked in quite exhausted. I don't think my friends know now that they nearly had to go home one short.

The Australians are reasonably kind to touring teams in the way they set out to entertain them. They don't overload the team with receptions, and they give them time to make personal friends and enjoy their times off the field.

*The incident that made Test history. Meckiff dramatically run out with the scores level and only two balls to go in the first Test at Brisbane, 1960, between Australia and the West Indies*

We are not quite so obliging to them in England, and put them through a terrific social whirl immediately on arrival in London. Two receptions daily get them introduced to everyone they ought to know in London, but they might well be given more time to make their own friends.

There was talk only a few years ago that cricket in Australia might die a natural death. Attendances were dropping sharply at Sheffield Shield games, and boys were enjoying games like tennis, golf, sailing and swimming, which give greater personal satisfaction and take up a lot less of the player's time.

Since then Australia have had the stimulating influence of Richie Benaud, the fantastic tie against the West Indies, the first ever in Test cricket, and many other cricketing feats to fire the imagination of the young cricketer.

Australia without cricket would not be the same country, and thank goodness their excellent Prime Minister, Mr Menzies, holds the same opinion.

## Chapter 7

# THE BEST OF COUNTY CRICKET

I HARDLY need to apologize for putting Sussex at the top of my list of counties when I write of performances that have impressed me and players whose personalities have made their work—players from whom I have tried to learn a bit about the game.

From Worthing there came to the Sussex County Club a diminutive, but well-built, all left-handed cricketer called Ken Suttle. This note about being *all* left-handed is quite important. Many left-handers bowl and throw right-handed, and this always means to me that they are not really natural left-handers. You have to be completely left-handed to satisfy me that you are a natural left-hander.

Ken Suttle kicks with his left foot at soccer (some say he doesn't know he has a right foot), and eats his meals, writes and waves goodbye with his left hand. If ever there was a natural at cricket it must be Ken Suttle. At one time his uncanny eye for a ball made him an unorthodox batsman. He scorned the normal shots for which fieldsmen were placed. He cut and pulled the ball from the wrong length and wrong place in the wrong direction. He exasperated every bowler he faced, enough for them to be glad to see the back of him if his audacious play betrayed him early in an innings.

As the years passed, with an M.C.C. trip to the West Indies behind him, a new maturity came to his batting. His record over the past three seasons has been amazingly consistent. He has found his ideal place in a good batting side at number three, and talking of records, he has gone very close to, if not beaten, the record for consecutive appearances for the county. He never wants to miss

97

*Ken Suttle. A natural cricketer*

a game of any description.

It is a tribute to his courage and determination that inevitable injuries have never kept him out of action long enough to see him on the sidelines in the next game. A top edge from a lifting ball from Statham hit him on the bridge of the nose and broke it, but he never missed a game.

A bad knee, finally diagnosed as cartilage trouble during the winter of 1961–2, was dealt with soon enough to keep that run of consecutive county appearances intact.

I nearly forgot to mention his bowling, and he would never have forgiven me. Lists of distinguished batsmen have fallen to his innocuous-looking but well-directed slows. Many a stubborn partnership has been broken and a game won by the simple words, 'Come on, Kenny, have a bowl.'

And I must not forget his halcyon days of boundary fielding when he had the pavilion crowd roaring their appreciation as, with a great sense of timing, he would just get to the ball one-handed and pitch it back over the top of the stumps.

Is it lack of inches, and a certain lack of style, that has kept him from representing England? Who knows, he still might. Nothing would surprise me from the really remarkable cricketer who is Kenneth George Suttle.

Yorkshire must, in the natural circle of things, come second to Sussex. A few years ago I suppose I would have written the same thing about Surrey during their long reign as County Champions. But Yorkshire are back at the top, and I don't grudge them that position in the least. Yorkshire is still the real home of cricket in England. The only place where husbands leave their families as by right, to watch the Yorkies at home.

One of the people most closely connected with Yorkshire's return to the top of the championship table has been Vic Wilson. He has had a very talented but young side to captain, and his experience has been invaluable to that side when things seemed to be going wrong. I have thought of him sometimes as a person sent to torment me on the occasions when I have captained Sussex or representative sides against Yorkshire.

Time and time again I have thought I had Yorkshire in trouble, particularly when they have batted badly. Then in walks Vic Wilson. As often as not, I find myself bowling at the time. I know I will get a few past the bat, but somehow he gets through the uncertain beginning, and starts to make runs. With the coolest possible head, he shields the weaker players from the better bowling, and Yorkshire again move out of trouble, guided safely by 'Big Vic'.

He is a big man, and has hands to go with his size. He catches extremely well, either in the slips or at short leg, and the faster they go, the easier he catches them. Bullet-like catches that would part my hands like leaves, bang safely into Vic's unyielding grasp.

His tactical sense has always been excellent, and he gave nothing away on the field that I can remember.

He has decided to retire from first-class cricket—as he said to me—'While I can still put up a decent show and not let the side down.' Typical of a man who never realized his worth to a side or, if he did, never talked about it. I wish him all the luck in the world as he continues his life as a farmer.

Across the country lies another great home of cricket, the Lancashire County Cricket Club. Old Trafford has been a happy hunting ground for me over the years. It was to play in their centenary match in 1957 that I had to ask my college tutor at Cambridge permission to miss examinations.

It was the most important invitation to play for a representative side that I had received, but it also clashed with second-year exams at the University designed to make certain I deserved to stay for a third year.

I don't know what prompted my tutor to put cricket first on this occasion, but he let me go, and I have been grateful ever since. I saw Len Hutton bat and even had him at the other end for one ball. I was so overcome at batting with such a great player that I lofted one into the covers to be caught out—bowled Hutton, rather than by the actual bowler.

I have enjoyed my every visit to Old Trafford, and have made plenty of runs there. One good reason may be the excellent sight screens at both ends.

At one end of Lord's there is a magnificent sight screen; at the other, the background is red-brick and black window spaces into which the old ball merges perfectly. The same situation exists at the Oval, and on many other grounds. At Old Trafford they had the decency to put the pavilion out of harm's way at the side of the ground and so allow the batsmen a good sight of the ball. Quite intelligent people these Lancastrians.

They are certainly very hospitable to southerners like myself, and make certain that visitors are looked after both at the ground and even on the Sunday of a Test Match. Invitations to golf and swim at the Mere Country Club, to cocktails at one house, to dinner at another, are always plentiful and much appreciated.

I played my first Test Match at Old Trafford, so it has special memories for me, despite the rain that washed out half of the match. It would be obvious to talk of Cyril Washbrook, though I never saw him at his best, or of Brian Statham, but I want to discuss another brilliant, but not so well-known Lancashire player, Ken Grieves. He was recently appointed captain of the side, so I anticipate some fine battles now that we are in direct opposition.

*Ken Grieves takes yet another slip catch. He can do it even with his eyes shut!*

My first taste of his batting ability came at Fenners. I had made 185, which seemed good enough to me, but Ken overshadowed that completely, making more than 200. It seemed he could square cut almost anything. Bowl a good length ball just outside the off stump, and he would crash it away square with a cross bat, and with so much power, that one boundary fielder was not enough. Pitch the ball up a bit, I thought, and he may still try to cut, but then his bat came upright, and, still half on the back foot, he would drive straight and through the covers with the best of them. He was a real terror to bowl to on a good wicket and quite capable of looking after himself on one that helped the bowlers more.

He was also a brilliant catcher of the ball. One evening, conversation had been intense on the subject of catching close to the wicket until finally Ken asked the assembled company the final question, 'Who is the best catcher in England?' Lock was the popular choice, but Ken had no doubts. 'You're wrong,' he replied, 'I am.' Said in good spirits with no hint of conceit, he was probably quite right. Caught Grieves bowled Greenhough was a common form of dismissal for a couple of seasons.

Skiers he liked to catch over his head as though bellowing through cupped hands to some friend out of easy hearing, standing a few feet above him. At practice he would ask someone to hit a real 'steepler'. He would judge its flight perfectly, lie down flat on the ground, and catch it bang in front of his face! Try it sometime, but don't forget to take off your glasses and remove your false teeth first!

Catching the ball high in front of the face is sometimes known as the Australian method. It may originate from their Australian rules football, where high catching two-handed is as important as kicking and running. This method avoids that blind spot where the eyes cannot follow the falling ball any further into the hands held at chest height. Brian Statham, Tom Graveney and many other good catchers take the ball the Australian way when they can, but perhaps the best advertisement for this method is Ken Grieves, who makes it look like child's play. I have recently started to catch this way, and don't remember dropping one. I am quite convinced that except for catches taken on the run, it is worth getting into a position to catch high in front of the face with the elbows turned outward, and the thumbs together, rather than in the accepted text-book way.

Coming south through the Midlands, we are likely to play a match against Leicestershire at the pleasant country grounds at Loughborough or Ashby-de-la-Zouch.

My first encounter with Leicestershire was on a victorious note at Cambridge. This labelled them as a sporting club for they made a generous declaration which enabled us to win. The second encounter labelled them as no respecter of reputations. The Sussex batting order was studded with international players, Sheppard, Doggart, Dexter, Suttle, Parks, Oakman, Smith, and yet, on a wet wicket, hardly one of us was allowed to reach double figures. The match was rained off which further labelled the county as a gentlemanly one, not wanting to embarrass their southern visitors more than was strictly necessary.

Loughborough was my old family home at the turn of the century, and so it was with pride that I made a hundred there in front of quite a few elderly people who knew me as the grandson of one of the locals.

There is plenty of interest in cricket in Leicestershire, and it has become the final resting place for more than one county player who has been pushed out of the top of his own county side by the urgent youth at the bottom, and it is of one such that I want to say a few words.

I first remember bowling to Alan Wharton when he was still with Lancashire in their Centenary match. It was a beauty of a wicket, and I was congratulating myself on a couple of maiden overs when Len Hutton called from the slips, 'Pitch it up a bit, and you might get a wicket.' Alan was an old enough soldier not to let such first-hand information go wasted, and as I pitched the ball up

*Benaud catching Trueman 'Australian fashion' with the hands in front of the face and*
**elbows turned out**

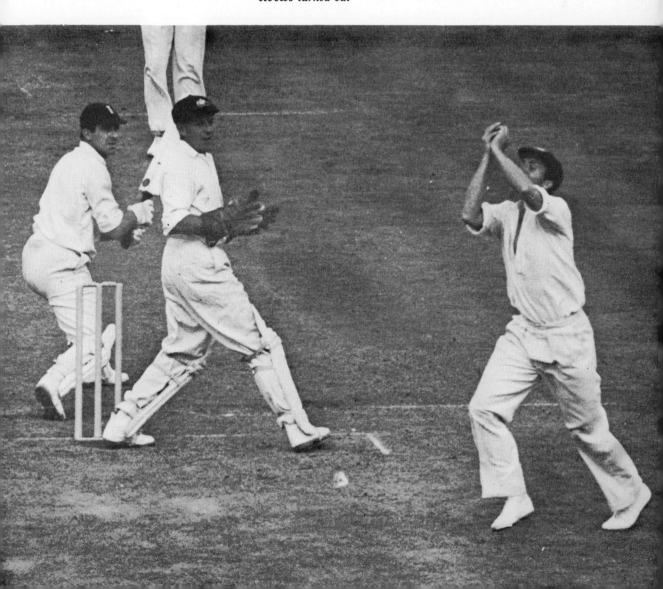

so he moved forward and drove me to all parts of the ground. Outside the off stump his foot was seldom to the ball, but he hardly ever picked the wrong one to drive.

Alan had never made a double century in his life, but on a warm day at Hove against Sussex he reached the awe-inspiring figure of 199. He pushed the next ball straight to cover, and was off like a jack rabbit for the other end. He was rightly sent back by the other batsman, while Ken Suttle (of all people to take a short run to) was picking it up.

Alan slipped on the turn going flat on his back on the green grassy verge to the wicket. The ball was on the wing to the 'keeper as he picked himself up and made a despairing dive back into his crease, covering his whole front with the mud and dust of the bowler's foot marks. The bails were off while he was in the air and the umpire gave him out.

Never a more dejected figure ever walked from the middle at Hove. There was surely not a soul present who was secretly not a little sorry that such a stalwart cricketer should have missed so great a milestone by so little.

Moving from Lancashire to Leicestershire didn't disturb Alan in any way. It rejuvenated him. Together with Willie Watson, who had made a similar move from Yorkshire, he bolstered the county batting with a constant and prolific flow of runs. Alan is an evergreen, and will be making his fair share of runs next year, and for a few years to come, while Leicestershire can continue to congratulate themselves on their good choice of other counties' cast-offs.

Talking of evergreens, the keen cricketer's mind jumps immediately away from the Midlands to the West Country where Somerset carry on an excellent cricketing campaign every year. They have been labelled a Commonwealth eleven, having imported Australian cricketers Colin McCool and Bill Alley, and Peter White from British Guiana. No batsman can help liking a visit to Taunton, where a small ground and friendly wicket combine in his favour, but most cricketers have enjoyed their games against Somerset over the last few years for the good humour and lively cricket that the Australians have inevitably produced.

Colin McCool seemed to take particular pleasure in making runs against Sussex and was the particular scourge of our skipper, Robin Marlar. Robin would bowl straight and get hit mercilessly on the leg side—he would bowl wider on the off side, and Colin would get his square driving and cutting into full working order. Robin might pursue his off side theory and try to block Colin's shots on the off side, but all to no avail—Colin would start hitting from off to leg just as safely, and Robin had to give him best again.

Colin was no fool with the ball either, and bowled his leg breaks for

Australia before his appointment to Somerset. He enjoyed his bowling as much as batting, and never stinted the batsman's runs if he had half a chance of getting a wicket.

I remember hitting him for fours and sixes as he continued to lay the bait. Sure enough, he had me stumped yards down the wicket, and that was the way he wanted it. He had some tricky balls up his sleeve, one of which had the same effect as Dooland's or Benaud's 'flipper'. I was nearly deceived by this 'skid on' ball more than once before I noticed that he held it differently, nearer the little finger, and more in the palm. From then on I relished the sight of the different grip: it was like backing a winner before it had gone past the post.

There is a temptation to be too clever when you know, or think you know, what the next ball will be. Batsmen often boast that they can pick a bowler's googly, and yet they still get out to it. Just because you know what is coming doesn't mean that it can be hit for four or six, and the recognized googly should be played with just as much respect as the recognized leg break.

Bill Alley was nominated one of five cricketers of the year in *Wisden* for his performances in 1961, when Bill was well into his forties. I often think that first-class batsmen are apt to give up a bit too soon in their lives, and Jack Hobbs' record of more hundreds after 40 than before would bear me out. I see no reason why a high-class batsman should not make 50 the age to be aimed at before retirement. Young lads on the ground staff will disagree no doubt because vacancies in the first team would not come along very often if everyone went on that long.

The reason for most early retirements is, in fact, loss of form. At the age of 30, a selection committee will be prepared to turn a blind eye to a run of low scoring by a batsman who, they know, will strike form again, and who must have plenty of good cricket left in him. The same committee will not be so tolerant to the 40-year-old, and a similar run of low scores must raise the question—'Don't you think we should give one of the youngsters a trial? He doesn't move as quickly as he used to.' These question marks will come up against our older player, who may well be persuaded of his waning powers long before he need be.

But no question of waning powers is raised in connection with Bill Alley. He not only bats better after his fortieth birthday, but bowls better as well. Did his 1961 season come from greater experience in his maturity? Was it a sudden new confidence among so many younger players that turned him over-night into the most prolific batsman in the country? He certainly never changed his well-known subjects and method of conversation whether he was taking wickets, making 3,000 runs or only 30.

*Bill Alley claims another victim as he knocks back Peter May's off stump*

Some of his more violent outbursts against bowlers who get him out luckily or against batsmen who misuse his bowling, are technicolor standard, plus a little highlighting of his own.

He bowls medium pace swingers and cutters, and is the very devil to score quickly against if he cares to bowl defensively. His left-hand batting sometimes defies the rules, but he defies them successfully for hours on end, so perhaps the rules are out of step, and not Bill Alley. He has renewed his contract with Somerset, and I for one am looking forward to seeing and listening to more of Bill in the next few years.

Nearby, in that lovely West Country, the Gloucestershire County Cricket Club have their headquarters at Bristol. Their cricket since I have known them has been largely regulated by the wicket on the Bristol ground, which, though it often produces results and good competitive cricket, is not the sort of wicket any groundsman would prepare by choice.

Prepared with only a little top grass, the ball soon turns, but slowly, and always low, demanding a steady forward play with little opportunity for proper stroke making. A lot more grass left on the top can make the ball move quickly off the seam for a day or so, but the surface goes dead and unresponsive after that, which is not much more satisfactory. The earth is just not the right consistency and no amount of rolling will make the sort of firm wicket found on clay soils.

In other countries, completely foreign soils are often imported to make big ground wickets, where the natural turf is unsatisfactory. In Sydney, Australia, they have recently laid a completely new surface of Bulli soil.

One match played in Kalgoorlie in 1962 was played on soil imported from many miles away, and what a beauty of a wicket it produced. That particular strip is used only a few times a year, and a good soaking, rolling and cutting brings it up as good as new each time. This may be the answer for wickets like the one at Bristol.

There have been two players from Gloucester, however, who rose above these difficulties to be the best possible stroke players. I only know of Wally Hammond by hearsay, but I watched and played against George Emmett in the last two or three years before his retirement. He is the sort of player I would like to be in my heart of hearts. He was small and quick, with lithe power in every movement. He was like a panther on to the ball as he flicked, slashed and tickled it all over the ground. For a few balls at the beginning of an innings he would look rather ordinary, but that was before his feet started to move properly. Once they started getting into the right places, there was no knowing where the ball would go next.

Twenty-five minutes at the end of the day held no terrors for George Emmett. No question of playing out time and starting properly the next morning. 'No time like the present' seemed to be his motto, and he liked to have twenty or thirty on the board to go to bed with. I know of no better sleeping pill for a cricketer than a few on the board overnight and the prospect of more to come in the morning. George Emmett probably slept sounder than most, because he was going to get more than his fair share on the morrow.

We might stay over that side of England for a minute to visit Glamorgan. It always seems to be a bit of a trek to play them in their native haunts, for they believe in taking cricket to the most far flung parts of their county. But the journey seems worth it when their unfailing hospitality gets under way, and the journey home again seems longer than ever.

*The classic balance and poise of George Emmett*

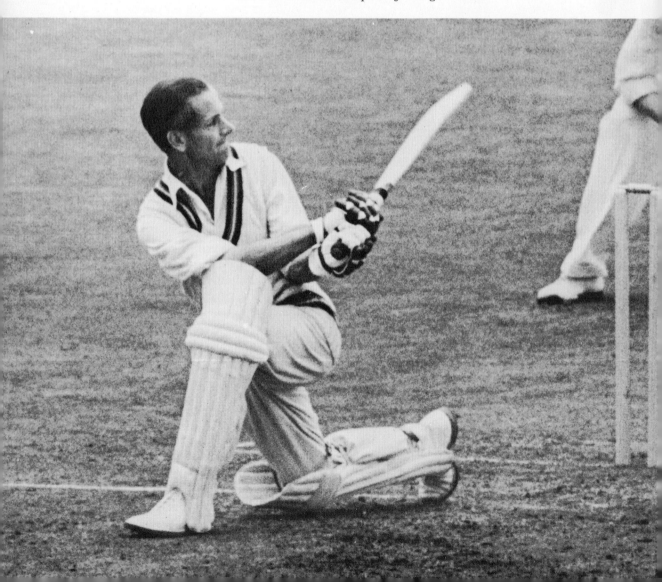

*Wilf Wooller. The nicest man in the world off the field, and the most unrelenting opponent on it*

They have been guided in their destiny during recent years by the strong and inimitable hand of Wilfred Wooller. The nicest man in the world off the field, and the most unrelenting opponent on it.

I could not believe it when I won my first contest against Wilf as captains of our respective counties. He had seemed a legendary character whose personality and strength could gain victory for his side when all odds were against them. It is an enviable reputation to have. His days as an international rugby player are still remembered all over Wales. Not least by the hotel whose grand piano was reputedly dropped a few floors to see if it would bounce.

The more I write of Wilf the more I realize that tales of his toughness on the cricket field and tales of wild rugby escapades are always second-hand. Nobody has actually been involved on these occasions, but they know someone who was. Perhaps these stories grow up about people who are really larger than life.

My own dealings with Wilf were as a player, under a selection committee of which he was a member, and they have always been very cordial. I enjoy reading his comments on rugby, which are always well informed and informative, and it will be a loss to county cricket if and when he leaves its administration.

A player to watch from those parts goes by the ubiquitous Welsh name of Jones. He bowls left arm over the wicket and is about twice as quick as he looks. He starts a little awkwardly in his run up, but gets smoother and more athletic with every stride. So many bowlers can look the part in the run and disintegrate as they try to bowl the ball. Ivor Jones is quite the opposite and, by the time he lets the ball go, you know you have seen a very fine bowling action. He has a terrific arm from the boundary, is young and keen to learn.

Some of those slow wickets in Wales might dampen his enthusiasm a little, but he should remember that half the county matches are played away from home, and he will get a bowl at Hove every couple of years! Seriously, I hope he can be handled well and encouraged, because a good left-arm fast bowler would be worth his weight in gold to England, particularly overseas on good wickets, where their surprise factor to batsmen accustomed mainly to right-arm bowlers is immeasurable.

Frank Tyson—'Typhoon Tyson'—this was the name that every newspaper carried for a couple of years in cricket's history. Tyson's name flashed like a meteor across the night sky, unheralded, then suddenly strong and brilliant and finally fading almost as quickly.

He was hardly a known force in English cricket when, with less than a hundred wickets to his name in the 1954 home season, he was selected to tour Australia with the M.C.C. There must have been many critics of that selection, just as there was probably less than 100 per cent agreement in the committee room, but that committee had been inspired into making the one selection that brought the Ashes back to England, almost a single-handed effort by the one fast bowler.

I was not even in England in those years, but followed the series in Australia keenly enough from the jungles of Malaya, where National Service had taken me. I would dearly love to have seen Frank at his fastest, bowling so fast that batsmen were beaten by the sheer pace and not the great skill of the bowler or by movement of the ball.

Australian batsmen were bowled by full tosses halfway up the stumps when they were still halfway through their stroke. My first personal encounter with Tyson was at the Scarborough Festival in 1957. I had made no runs in three

'Typhoon' Tyson

previous innings, but I had enjoyed the festival enough to want to ensure an invitation for the following year.

I begged to be allowed to open the batting, and found one of the intended opening batsmen holding his head, either through actual illness or just that particularly painful sort which follows a full evening of Scarborough's special hospitality. He was happy to let me go in against an attack containing Tyson and Trueman.

Fast bowlers have normally had enough by the time festival matches are played in September, and I made nearly a hundred before lunch. I got out in the last over before the interval trying to hit Trueman for six to complete my century—not very good tactics, but it would have been fun if it had come off. I remember even hooking Frank Tyson, but thinking that I might not want to try it against him on either a quicker wicket or when he was a bit fresher.

It was the next year at Scarborough that I saw Frank at his quickest, probably not so fast as he had been in his great year in Australia, but still something very much out of the ordinary. He had just been picked to tour Australia again in 1958, and again there was strong criticism of this selection. I think he was determined to show everyone at the ground that he was still a force to be reckoned with.

I was standing in the slips and Godfrey Evans was keeping wicket. The first ball was let go outside the off stump and was still on the rise as Godfrey took it, jumping in the air to soften the impact. We all looked at each other in amazement and retired about three yards further back. It was the first time I had ever hoped that a catch would not come my way, not from any fear of dropping it, but from pure physical fear that it might well hit me before I could get my hands there, or even break a finger on the way.

It may have been the slow turning wickets prevalent in Northants at that time, wickets which suited their high-class spinners, Jack Manning and George Tribe, which shortened the effective fast bowling life of Tyson so drastically. By 1959 his pace had all but gone, and he modified his action to try to get more movement. A season or two of that, and he decided to quit the cricketing scene, to leave England, and to settle in his charming wife's home town in Australia, where he now lives happily with a growing family.

Now Northants have another fine fast bowling prospect in the giant David Larter. The home wickets are rather quicker now with continual demands from the authorities to prepare the best possible fast wickets for county cricket. Larter should have plenty of opportunities to use pace and height which were denied to Frank Tyson. I hope he takes every advantage of them, and is as successful as was the other genial giant before him.

Not far away from Northants lies the sprawling area of Birmingham. In one of the more attractive suburbs at Edgbaston, the Warwickshire County Cricket Club flourishes as never before. Their supporters' pool has grown so quickly and to such proportions that a brand new building, more like a city centre bank, was rushed up to house its workings.

They say that Ray Hitchcock started the pool and could have maintained a small percentage personal interest in it had he so wished. That would be big money now, for they are dealing with hundreds of thousands of members. The money is being well spent in providing England with one of its finest cricket grounds. The ground is administered admirably by Leslie Deakin, and together with his assistant secretary and captain, Mike Smith, they form a formidable organization.

Mike Smith has been a thorn in every bowler's side from time to time, and there is usually not long to wait before he makes you pay for getting him out

*Mike Smith rolls over, but hangs on to complete a fine catch, and out goes Trevor Goddard off Statham's bowling*

cheaply. Mike is a thoughtful cricketer, and has exploited the old idea that if you bowl at the off-stump, fielders are needed on the off side. He has further exploited the leg side limitation of only five fielders and I believe his liking for leg side play is the result of clear thinking about the new lbw rule and the leg side limitation of fielders.

He has records without number to his name. Records at school, records in university matches, records in first-class cricket—but a less brilliant career in Test Matches. It is said that he is vulnerable to quick bowling early in an innings, but who isn't? It is suggested that his glasses make it difficult for him in very bright sunlight. A variety of such reasons are given for his lesser success in Test cricket, yet one should not forget his two big innings for England in the West Indies, though these were interspersed with lower scores. Nor should one forget his 99 at Lahore against Pakistan which won England the match and the series in 1961.

But generally I believe Mike Smith's temperament is not ideally suited to Test cricket, where time plays no great part. Mike is at his best on a difficult wicket when things are against him and time is running out. He thinks his way brilliantly through this sort of situation, and I would pick him above all others for the bumping pitch, the blinding light and the last-man-in situation. He hits leg spinners to leg for the good reason that there are fewer fielders that side. If he does it successfully enough to get the opposing captain to split his field, there will be that many more gaps on the off side, and he will score through there with the best will in the world.

He made 160-odd for the Gentlemen against the Players when hardly another player made double figures. We watched in admiration from the dressing-room. He played the best bowlers in England on a bad wicket as though they were schoolboys giving him practice on a beauty. I have felt that he almost scorns to play a long innings on a good wicket against defensive bowling—which is a large part of Test batsmanship. He likes to have something to play for, something to think about, to get his teeth into, and only then is the best seen of one of the most remarkable batsmen of our time.

County batsmen are inclined to talk more quietly or laugh a little louder about less funny jokes as they get near Derbyshire to play an away match. For the last ten years one name has been on their minds. The best bowler I have ever faced—Les Jackson.

The first time he bowled at me was at Fenners on a beautiful batsman's wicket. I had no idea who he was, and played him happily enough until I got out. I seem to remember he took more than ten wickets in the match, but I thought no more about it.

*'Jacko'—the best bowler I have ever faced*

The next meeting was at Derby when the laugh was really on me. The wicket was green, grassy and hard, when Donald Carr won the toss and asked Sussex to bat. One or two wickets fell to Jackson, but I walked quite confidently to the middle.

No two balls did the same thing, and hardly a straight one was bowled.

They bent one way in the air and broke back off the wicket as though controlled on a string. I decided that the one way to survive was to play only to keep my wicket intact, and hope to tire the great man out. I let them hit me on the pads when just outside leg stump, and let them go by within inches of the off stump. Jackson soon banged one down and as I saw it hit the wicket short and a foot outside the off stump, I shouldered arms expecting to see it fly harmlessly by. The next moment I dropped my bat involuntarily as the ball cracked me on the point of the left elbow. It had come back off the wicket like an off break, and even Jackson had the grace to say that he didn't think 'even he could move it that much'.

I was rather ashamed at dropping my bat, and when the fielders asked me whether I was OK I made the rash statement 'I'll be all right after the next ball'. I was, indeed, because the middle stump was flying out of the ground, and I was able to lick my wounds in the comfort of the dressing-room.

'Jacko' has been called a slinger and was unlucky enough to come to his best at the same time as Trueman, Statham and Tyson. He might have played for England for ten years had he got the chance as a younger man. He has played only once for England in recent years, and it was largely due to him that England won the game.

I had always thought of him as a superb bowler in helpful conditions, but that first day at Leeds against Australia, he proved me only half aware of his great ability. On a slow wicket he bowled with deadly accuracy to keep the scoring down on the first day. The wicket was bound to turn later in the match and it was vital to keep scoring to a minimum until the spinners could do their work. It was a brilliant piece of bowling which was worth many wickets to England as the game progressed.

Every year the county batsmen say hopefully 'Jackson won't be so fast this year'—'not so good this year'—or even more hopefully 'won't be playing this year'. But each year there he is with the new ball in his hand, and devil take you if you don't look sharp and bat your best.

The Worcestershire County Cricket Club have the honour to entertain any touring side to England for their first match of the tour. It is always an exciting moment when new players from overseas are on view for the first time, and for many keen followers this game is the goal for an annual pilgrimage. They

*The beautiful County Ground at Worcester—a magnificent setting for cricket*

journey to see new players and be reminded of the skills of those they have known well before, but also to see the beginning of a new season, and remember the attractions of the cricket ground with river and cathedral in the background.

The playing area is probably flooded at some stage every winter, and the river has been kind in this respect. Over the years, the wickets at Worcester have provided excellent games of cricket. A fast outfield has made for good-looking shots and has given the opportunity for more than one fielder to make a reputation for himself.

In 1962 the club nearly won the County Championship, and had they done so it would have been a just reward for their excellent captain, Don Kenyon. Needing fourteen points in their last match to have a chance of beating Yorkshire the whole side responded magnificently under Don's leadership, to win the game and be ten points clear of Yorkshire before the northern club's final match.

On a wicket that had had rain on it during the match, Don Kenyon played a true captain's innings to make a hundred and win the game. He has always believed in hitting the ball hard, and in recent years seems to like to hit the first ball he receives for four.

There is certainly a good opportunity for opening batsmen against the new ball to get quick runs, while the fielders are still in attacking positions. I particularly remember those pleasant times when I have had runs on the board and the fielding side have taken the new ball. They feel they must take advantage of its newness and have the fielders close in catching positions. The ball is new and that much easier to see, and it is a glorious chance to score freely. It must be the same for every opening batsman if he can be confident enough to have a go.

Don Kenyon never lacked confidence as a batsman and has passed on his method of playing to most of those he has played with in Worcester. Martin Horton, Dick Richardson and Ron Headley are all good strikers of the ball and get their runs in a most attractive way. They probably owe much of their skill to Don Kenyon's example.

Five years ago Don was one of the most prolific batsmen in county cricket. He has a lot of double centuries to his name, and seldom has a hundred taken him more than three hours to make. He reckons that a good wicket can reduce the finest bowlers in the world to the same level, and that is exactly what he used to do when that Worcester ground had a few years of really good wickets.

'Bring them down here, and we'll see who can bowl and who can't, Matey.' 'Matey' is his general term of address for all cricketers young and old, famous and unknown. It is part of the generous nature of a fine cricketer, and excellent county captain, who has had a vigorous influence on the game throughout his career.

I remember Trent Bridge in Nottingham for one unhappy moment against the South Africans in 1960. England needed only thirty-odd runs to win the match on an overcast morning with rain threatening. South Africa's opening bowlers started as though they were determined to bowl us out for twenty. Raman Subba Row and the other opener withstood the attack admirably until one of them got out. England needed only one run to win.

What a miserable walk I had to the wicket to play the last ball of an over from Trevor Goddard. It swung in, hit me on the pads, but a loud appeal was turned down by the umpire.

'Thank goodness for that,' I thought, 'now I can watch Raman get the winning run at the other end.'

Adcock was bowling at a terrific speed and Raman was lucky to keep his wicket intact let alone get the winning run.

Soon enough, I was facing Trevor Goddard again. Each ball was a perfect length moving in a little, with no chance of a run, as the field crowded closer. The last ball was just down the leg side, and I swung heartily at it in relief. Alas, not the meat of the bat, but the top edge hit the ball, and I was caught at square leg for o.

One to win, and I got nothing—and not the only duck I got either, because I was soon the proud possessor of various ties sent to me through the post patterned with all manner and sizes of duck.

I felt even more sorry as I passed Ken Barrington on the pavilion steps. He made exactly the same remark to me as I had made on my way to the wicket: 'Thank you very much!'

Raman and I had crossed while the ball was in the air—had it been dropped we would have had the winning run, but since it was the last ball of the over poor Ken Barrington had to face the first ball of an over from Adcock.

The first ball was a perfect length just outside the off stump, a little snick and the ball flew to first slip—he dropped it, it ran through his legs, and a scampered run made England the winners. What a nightmare it was for those concerned, and think of the feelings of the poor chap who was next in after Ken!

I enjoy journeys to Nottingham, but particularly since the most jovial cricketer in England has joined the county club. Bomber Wells had some years with Gloucester before moving north. He is the off spinner with the shortest run up, the biggest variety of balls to bowl (including a well-pitched leg break), the happiest sense of humour and the biggest heart in the game.

His sense of fun has almost got the better of him on occasions. Some might think it rather overdoing things to hit the batting Brigadier in the ear with a jet from a water pistol from gully in a Services match, but Bomber could not resist the temptation, nor could he stop laughing for some time afterwards.

He is a real enthusiast for the game, and cares not a jot how many wickets he gets so long as the cricket is entertaining to the public. He believes that cricket is a batsman's game, and it should be played on perfect wickets, and that the occasional wicket taken by slow bowlers should be suitably rewarded. He is the one batsman in county cricket whose style of play never changes from year to year. He delivers a lusty mow at each ball with a cross bat and enough skill to decide whether it should fly over extra cover, the bowler, or in his favourite spot, 'cow-shot corner'. He never stops his tricks as a bowler, delivering the odd ball from behind the umpire, always ready to bowl before the batsman is looking, but never taking unfair advantage of the fact.

In a tight game he can be really skilful as a bowler, but he will still laugh if he gets half a chance.

You might think that Trevor Bailey was at the opposite end of the scale from Bomber Wells in his approach to the game, but a more realistic appraisal of Trevor Bailey would be as one of the best all-round cricketers of our time, rather than as a stonewalling defensive type of cricketer.

The best of Trevor's cricket is surely as a bowler. He bowls very close to the stumps, his arm higher than anyone else in the game, and making full use of his height.

To captain Essex, make two thousand runs and take more than a hundred wickets in a season would put any young player almost automatically into the running for a Test cap, but that is what Trevor Bailey did in 1961 when he had finished playing international cricket.

When not touring with the M.C.C. in the winter his business commitments are numerous, and he finds it difficult to contain his weight. At the beginning of the new season he spends all his time in track suits running off those extra pounds, and hardly has time to get into the nets.

Come the first match, he naturally takes the new ball and pitches it bang on a length. He is off again on his marathon season of batting and bowling his side out of tight corners, and to well-deserved victories.

Under his captaincy Essex always seem a hard side to beat, especially on their home grounds. They have no headquarters ground, but play their home programme on park grounds, owned and prepared by the municipalities. The wickets are often a bit lively, and those Essex batsmen never waste much time if they are going to make runs.

Trevor often has to get them out of trouble if the aggression, which he encourages, lands his early batsmen in the cart. You have only to watch Gordon Barker and Barry Knight to realize that, for all Trevor's defensive skill, he doesn't consider defence as the only way to play the game. He even hit a six at Worthing against Sussex this summer!

Immediately after the Second World War, London was starving, not for food, though that had been in short supply for some years, but for first-class cricket, and all that it meant to so many people. Members of the M.C.C. had been deprived of their normal summer entertainment, of their quiet club life at

*Trevor Bailey, proving he is not purely a defensive batsman*

Lord's, drinks at the bar, snoozes on the front benches, arguments about the merits of the players in the middle, and of those who played there years before.

Those arguments must have grown pretty warm between the young and old, when Denis Compton, Bill Edrich and Jack Robertson were scoring thousands of runs in those post-war 'forties. Who was the best of the three was probably food for as good an argument as any, and if you saw the best innings played by any of them it must have been mighty difficult to choose.

Denis Compton was probably the most adaptable player of the three, and the one to show the most genius for the game. My school friend, co-member of the same cricket eleven and Middlesex county cricketer, Chris Walton, told me

*Denis Compton turns to leg*

of lending a new bat to Denis in the early season nets at Lord's. Denis seldom managed to have all his cricket gear together at the right time and at the right place, so replacement articles were usually in demand. The wicket was damp on this occasion, and difficult enough for the average player, particularly so early in the season. It was Denis's first knock of the season, and when he handed the bat back after twenty minutes the one muddy mark in the meat of the bat was the only proof of it having been used at all. To most of us that would prove that we had only made contact once. In Denis's hands it meant that every ball for twenty minutes had been struck sweetly in the middle, not a mark on the edge nor high up on the splice, but just the mark of perfect timing, where it ought to be.

Jack Robertson was the most refined batsman I have played against. Batting was reduced to its most economical limits in terms of movement, to a refinement only known to great artists. He never hit the ball hard, and yet beat the field easily to get his fours. He moved down the wicket to every ball of our slow bowlers at Cambridge, and scored off almost every one of them, if I remember correctly.

If he were to the pitch of the ball he would propel it effortlessly through the gaps between fielders. If he were not to the pitch of the ball he would be content to push it slowly for one and proceed unhurriedly to the other end. His hook shot was similarly calm and graceful. Most players like to hook hard, to swat the ball away from in front of their eyes, but Jack Robertson would sway inside and just help the ball on its way.

Can it be true that he played for England in the second Test against South Africa in 1949, made a hundred and was dropped for the rest of the series? It seems like a nightmare, and yet Jack would never mention the fact to anyone. He was making many runs at the same time as the 'terrible twins', Compton and Edrich, and must have felt the coldness of their shadow, but whether they scored more or less than he did, they never made them more elegantly.

Bill Edrich was the most forthright of the three. His shots on the leg side could reasonably be described as hits to leg rather than hooks, pulls or on drives. Bowlers aimed at his leg stump at their peril, and, whatever length the ball, it was treated with little ceremony. He was as tough as they come, and demonstrated his attitude admirably to me in the course of a cricketing conversation quite late one evening at Scarborough.

We were talking about fast bowlers and the merits of hooking them or leaving short balls alone. The question of getting hit on the head was raised, but he dismissed it summarily. 'Have you ever been hit on the head?' he asked me. I admitted to a glancing blow on the chin, and not much else. 'It doesn't

123

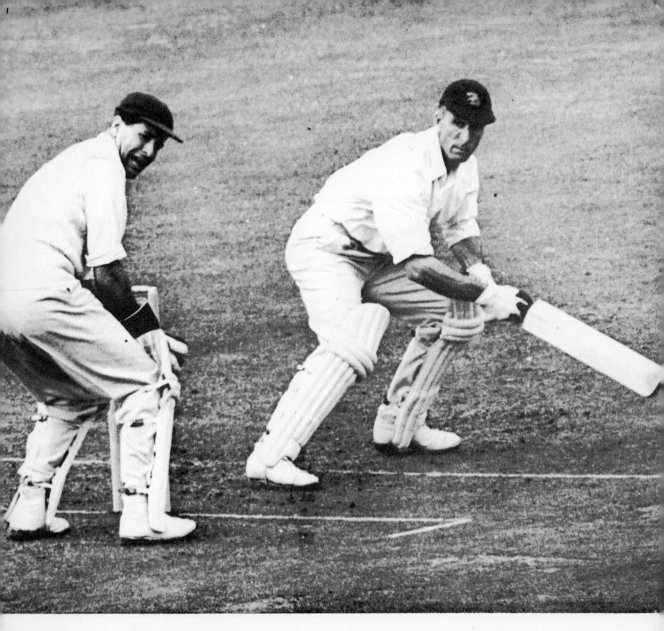

*Jack Robertson late cuts for 3, on his way to a century before lunch against Sussex*

hurt much anyway,' he concluded. He was hit in the face by Frank Tyson at
his fastest and was carried off, but was back batting on the following day,
letting the short balls bounce off his chest like a drum.

It seems wrong to dismiss these three great stalwarts of Middlesex and
Lord's in such a small space, but I will never forget the pleasure of seeing them

play.

Surrey won the County Championship seven years in succession, and fully deserved to. They had a Test class bowling side to suit any conditions they might meet in England. Alec Bedser and Peter Loader could move the new ball more than any bowler in the country, and if the wicket did not suit them then the great Laker-Lock partnership could take over where they left off. Some of the wickets at the Oval were rather soft and crumbly in those years, but Laker and Lock were just as successful in their away matches as at home.

I particularly remember Peter Loader bowling at Guildford one rather dark overcast day. Having bowled a series of beautifully controlled in-swingers and out-swingers which I kept out of my wicket, he let go a perfectly pitched bouncer. I had to duck quickly at the last second and split the seat of my trousers from end to end. I wondered whether to go off for running repairs and lose the thread of my innings, or to stay in the middle slightly exposed and feeling draughty. I chose the latter course, but it made little difference as Loader soon hit my middle stump with a well-disguised slow one coming in from the off.

My encounters with Alec Bedser have come out about fifty-fifty. He knocked my off stump out on the truest type of Oval wicket, but I got my revenge at Hove when he took the new ball later in the afternoon.

I resolved to have a hit at the first ball he swung in towards my body. He might have read my thoughts because for two overs he bowled straight at the off stump, and anything but good defence would have been too risky. Then in the next over came the old familiar in-swinger. I was fully prepared and swung at the ball as it moved in the air. The ball was found a few minutes later in the gardens adjoining the ground. Not a shot to be proud of or to practise, but a shot to remember as something a little out of the ordinary.

That Surrey side could have been one of the greatest in England's county history but for a slight weakness in the batting line-up. They had Peter May to provide the class and Bernie Constable to provide the experience, but Ken Barrington and Micky Stewart were only learning the game in those years, and could not be expected to be consistent. If Surrey's present batting side could have played with their earlier bowlers, what a combination they would have been. John Edrich, Micky Stewart, Ken Barrington and Peter May make a formidable array, and even Bernie Constable keeps on reappearing to make runs when his side needs them most.

Talking of reappearances, you should have seen Jim Laker bowling for Essex on his come-back to first-class cricket in 1962. Sussex were unlucky enough to meet him on a turning wicket in about his fifth game—just enough to get the great man back into practice.

Many other off spinners had bowled and been hit during that week at Worthing, but Jim Laker was of a different class altogether. He spun the ball so much that it would lift as well as turn, hit high on the bat instead of the meat, and turn a four into an easy catch at mid-wicket.

Tony Lock has, of course, started to bowl slower than in his heyday of two hundred wickets a season for Surrey. He is now an orthodox left-armer who varies his pace and flight very cleverly, but cannot be so completely demoralizing as he used to be.

I could write a book about Peter May both as a most brilliant batsman and as a most understanding and helpful captain. His retirement rather early from the Test match scene was deeply regretted by all the players who had known him, watched him and played under him. Nobody regretted that retirement more than myself to whom he had given the greatest help and encouragement all the way along the various stepping stones into international cricket.

Finally, I want to speak of a really good friend and the greatest international cricketer of the lot, Godfrey Evans. What an amazing man to look at—eyes so bright that they appeared to be always full of humour; an impression of tremendous physical strength which is no illusion; an obvious capacity for hard work, for enjoying life; and one of the best showmen cricket has ever known.

Come five o'clock on a hot day after five hours in the field, Godfrey was always the one to remember that the television had started to record the proceedings. 'Come on, lads, put on a show for the television!' and Godfrey would become the liveliest of the lot, including those players ten years his junior.

Colin Cowdrey often speaks of Godfrey's physical courage when standing up to Alec Bedser's bowling on wet wickets. He would stop the ball on his bare forearm and never wince nor take a moment to rub the place. His strong arms played a large part in his outstanding skill as a 'keeper. I am sure he could move a fist over eighteen inches considerably quicker than you or I, and could therefore catch that many more deflections behind the wicket.

I remember him taking a ball left-handed on the half volley just by the base of the leg stump and stumping the stumbling batsman in the same movement. He made it easy for the younger players in the England side to feel at home and part of the show. There was always the offer of a drink or a ride home in his Bentley, which I used to accept with pleasure.

Godfrey loved a party and lots of people to enjoy it with. Even now, when a champagne cork pops in a hotel dining-room, I turn round to see whether Godfrey is holding the bottle, roaring with laughter, and dispensing the bubbly to anyone who cares to drink it with him.

*Godfrey Evans grins characteristically as he drives Fred Titmus for 6 at Lord's*

Godfrey was such a law unto himself that it is proving a very difficult task for his successors to keep their place in the England side. It is impossible to watch an English 'keeper and not compare him with Godfrey at his best, so anything but brilliance appears second rate.

Time will no doubt fade the memory of Godfrey Evans, and another wicket-keeper will take on his mantle, but time will never dim my appreciation of his kindness to me as a young England cricketer, and I wish him all the luck in the world now that his unapproachable cricket career is ended.

I cannot think of a better subject on which to end my commentary on cricket in England and throughout the world. Cricket is a game that embraces the lives and cares of millions, but let us always remember that it is only a game. It just happens to be the best game in the world.

*Close of play*

128